Letting Go:

A Christian's Guide to Finding Peace in an Alcoholic Relationship

ABIGAIL STRONG

Cover design: Adam Young

No part of this book may be reproduced, stored in a retrieval system, or transmitted by any way or means: electronic, mechanical, photocopy, recording, or otherwise without prior permission from the author at Letting_Go_Book@yahoo.com.

The Twelve Steps are reprinted with permission of Alcoholics Anonymous World Services, Inc. ("AAWS") Permission to reprint the Twelve Steps does not mean that AAWS has reviewed or approved the contents of this publication, or that AAWS necessarily agrees with the views expressed herein. A.A. is a program of recovery from alcoholism only - use of the Twelve Steps in connection with programs and activities which are patterned after A.A., but which address other problems, or in any other non-A.A. context, does not imply otherwise. Additionally, while A.A. is a spiritual program, A.A. is not a religious program. Thus, A.A. is not affiliated or allied with any sect, denomination, or specific religious belief.

THE HOLY BIBLE, NEW INTERNATIONAL VERSION®, NIV® Copyright © 1973, 1978, 1984, 2011 by Biblica, Inc.® Used by permission. All rights reserved worldwide.

These Scriptures are copyrighted by the Biblica, Inc.® and have been made available on the Internet for your personal use only. Any other use including, but not limited to, copying or reposting on the Internet is prohibited. These Scriptures may not be altered or modified in any form and must remain in their original context. These Scriptures may not be sold or otherwise offered for sale.

These Scriptures are not shareware and may not be duplicated.

Copyright © 2014 Abigail Strong
All rights reserved.
ISBN-10: 1505302447
ISBN-13: 978-1505302448

DEDICATION

This book is dedicated to Mom and Pop, who taught me what true love is, my beloved children, who have always encouraged and supported me, to my best friend, Michael, who listened to me gripe about the virtues of putting in headers and footers, and to all my sisters and brothers out there seeking peace within an alcoholic relationship.

TABLE OF CONTENTS

Introduction 7

Part 1: Understanding the Disease 11

1 The Six Stages of Alcoholism 13
2 You Can't Reason with a Madman 18
3 Anger Fuels Alcoholism 23
4 The Dog, The Goldfish, or Whatever 27
5 Financial Ruin 31
6 Adultery 36

Part 2: Helping the Alcoholic 43

7 The Alcoholic's Confession 45
8 Intercessory Prayers 49
9 Praying for Healing 55
10 More on Prayer 59
11 Do's and Don'ts 64
12 Loving from the Top Down 72

Part 3: Helping Yourself 75

13 Have No Other Gods 77
14 Boundaries 81
15 Obsessive Thinking 88

16	Facing Loneliness	94
17	Self-Righteousness	99
18	Putting on the Full Armor of God	106
19	The Children	113
20	Choices	119
21	Finding Peace	128

Part 4: Recovering from Alcoholism — **135**

22	A Dry Drunk	137
23	Detox and Rehab	143
24	The Lost Son Returns	147
25	After Sobriety	152

Part 5: Moving Forward — **157**

26	Reconciliation	159
27	Decisions	163
28	Letting Go	168

Appendix A: Biblical Quotes	173
Appendix B: Helpful Websites	179
Appendix C: Phoning for Help	181
Appendix D: Dreams	183

INTRODUCTION

Come to me, all you who are weary and burdened, and I will give you rest. Take my yoke upon you and learn from me, for I am gentle and humble in heart, and you will find rest for your souls. For my yoke is easy and my burden is light. Matthew 11:28-30

If you are in a relationship with an alcoholic, believe that God loves that person as much as you do, and wants you to live in peace with that person, then this guide to understanding, dealing with it, healing, and finding peace in an alcoholic relationship was written specifically for you.

I was married to an alcoholic for twenty-seven years. There were good times and bad times. God blessed us with two wonderful children, and for the most part, I was deeply in love with my husband.

I was *not* in love with the alcohol. I abhorred it! It completely changed my husband's personality into someone I did not know. He embarrassed me. I was afraid of him. Eventually, the disease did its evil and insidious job, and my husband became a dangerous, irrational, disgusting man, whom I barely recognized — a mere shadow of his former self. Sadly, our marriage ended in divorce. This was not my choice, but that is how it happened.

I loved my husband. I really did. I hated what alcohol was doing to our marriage, our family, and him. I wanted to help. I needed this to stop or something terrible was going to happen. Thus began my quest for answers.

First, I began reading. I read my Bible and searched for texts on alcoholism. I bought books and checked out books from the library. There were plenty out there, but only one or two dealing with alcoholism from a Christian perspective, which is what I was really looking for.

I was not deterred. I read whatever I could get my hands on. This was not enough.

Next, I began attending meetings. This was hard for me to do at first, but I bit the bullet and attended them with fear and trepidation, being a newbie and all. I went to open AA meetings and Al-Anon meetings. These meetings were great in that they helped me understand the nature of alcoholism, but they offered little to no advice on dealing with alcoholics. I went to counseling and group therapy specializing in families living with chemically dependent members. I had counseling from the pastor at our church. My husband and I even went to a three different counselors together – sadly, all three of them said they could do nothing for him or us, until he got help with his alcoholism, which he denied he needed. These meetings were great. I was finally beginning to get some answers.

Finally, I began talking to people — all kinds of people. I talked with the some leading counselors in the field. I talked with alcoholics, wives, husbands, mothers, fathers, sons, and daughters of alcoholics. I spoke to God about alcoholics. I listened, and listened, and learned.

What resulted from all this research is the book you now hold in your hands. It is a compilation of everything I learned. You will find that it is not full of overly scientific or psychiatric theories — just plain common sense in an easy to read format laced with Biblical wisdom. I wish I had had this book while I was going through our difficult patches. It could have saved me from a lot of heartache.

What I do know is that God put it into my heart to write this book to be a blessing to others who are going through the same misery I went through. God be with you on your journey to find peace.

Important Notices:

- **I am NOT a counselor. All advice given in this book is for informational purposes only. Seek professional counseling before making any life changes.**
- Most of the chapters in this book were written while I was in the midst of my alcoholic marriage. I have chosen to leave it as written to capture the raw emotion felt during those rough times.

- This book applies to all chemically dependent relationships, not just alcoholic ones.
- I will refer to the alcoholic as "he" throughout the book in order to make it easier to read, but its principles apply equally to females.

PART 1:
UNDERSTANDING THE ALCOHOLIC

Part 1: Understanding the Alcoholic

1 THE SIX STAGES OF ALCOHOLISM

Wine is a mocker and beer a brawler; whoever is led astray by them is not wise. Proverbs 20:1

Understanding the stages of alcoholism has given me more empathy for my husband's battle over alcoholism; therefore, I'd like to share with you what I've learned. I have chosen to divide the progression into six stages with descriptions of what to look for within each step.

Stage 1: Social Drinking — This is the first stage of the downward spiral into alcoholism. It usually begins when someone offers him a drink. He takes the drink and likes it.

At this stage, the drinker will drink solely at social occasions. He is "in control" and prides himself in knowing that he will not make a fool of himself, as he has seen others do. He is not worried that he will drink more than he can handle.

Stage 2: Secretive Drinking — The drinker no longer drinks solely at social occasions, but begins to drink while alone. He begins to find reasons he needs a drink to unwind after a hard day at work, or to cool off after mowing outside. A nice cold one while watching the game on a Sunday afternoon is just what his nerves need.

This is really the first phase in which you will notice the drinker's personality begin to change. He becomes secretive and lies about the number of drinks he's had, when he drinks, and where he's been drinking. You will notice he will hastily gulp down alcohol in social situations.

1 The Six Stages of Alcoholism

Stage 3: Problem Drinking — At this point the drinker can control when he begins to drink, but can no longer control when he quits. He begins to binge drink.

It scares him that he is losing control. He realizes he has a problem, but doesn't know what to do about it. His pride keeps him from admitting he has a problem.

His life becomes fuzzy. He forgets where he's been and what he's done. Blackouts occur.

Stage 4: The Alcoholic – At this stage, you will see that there is a sudden, marked personality change. The problem-drinker has now become an alcoholic. He can no longer control his life, and his alcoholism begins to affect his relationships. He lies, wants to be alone, is selfish, and protective of his secretive alcoholic activities.

He will probably lose his job due to drinking, and refuses to take responsibility for his actions. He depends on the support of an enabler. This enabler may be his wife, his family, the community, or the government. Without them, he'd be homeless and living on the streets. Some do.

Don't think that he will be ashamed of what he is doing. Oh, no. He will be arrogant and prideful. He will refuse to admit there is anything wrong with what he is doing.

The funny thing is, the sicker he becomes, the more demanding he will be on those around him. He will demand perfection from his enablers, while overlooking the terrible mistakes he is making. The consequences of his actions will be blamed on others — not him.

This stage will be very difficult on those who love him.

Stage 5: Point of No Return — This stage is gradual. He continues to seesaw back and forth between getting and losing jobs. He has probably lost family and friends at this point. The drinker will feel that no one cares for him. That he is alone in the world. That all have turned against him.

In this stage the alcoholic may binge drink for many days or weeks always ending in delirium tremens.

He will probably be hospitalized for the first time due to some illness related to his drinking.

He is likely to be arrested for DUI, public intoxication, or some crime committed while under the influence.

Amazingly, through all of this, his sense of pride is unscathed. He will not admit to anyone that he has a problem. Instead, he will blame others for his social dilemmas and financial crises.

Stage 6: Physical Breakdown — In this final stage of alcoholism, the alcoholic no longer cares how he looks or smells. His clothes are wrinkled and filthy. He doesn't bother to comb his hair. His eyes are bloodshot. He stumbles, mumbles, and cries. He looks 20 years older than he actually is.

The healthy body God gave him has finally begun to break down under constant neglect and abuse. He may develop "wine sores," and his ears may bleed. His hands tremble. His liver is eaten up with cirrhosis and begins to shut down. He is malnourished and has nervous, mental, stomach, and intestinal problems.

His mind isn't what it used to be. He no longer can reason, complete, or understand simple math or logic-based problems. His short and long-term memory is shot.

He is no longer a good worker. He has long since given up on trying to find or hold down a job, and is, at this point, totally dependent on someone else for support.

I have been watching my husband's physical and mental deterioration over the past few years. Apparently, he experienced stage 1 as a teenager, before I met him; then underwent a spiritual awakening and quit drinking for number years. Sadly, about five years ago he returned to drinking again, thinking he could control it — stage 2. As I write this he has progressed to stage 5 of this hideous disease and may be entering stage 6, the final stage of organic deterioration.

I have not given up hope that he will someday recover. I pray for him several times a day. Family, friends and church members are praying for him to let go of his pride and come to Jesus. We are a faithful army. We will not give up.

God is my rock, my shield, and my salvation. He is with me, and will not let me down.

1 The Six Stages of Alcoholism

What stage of alcoholism do you believe your alcoholic to be in?

What makes you believe he is in this stage?

Part 1: Understanding the Alcoholic

Name the actions your alcoholic is displaying, which characterize this stage.

How have these actions affected your life?

2 YOU CAN'T REASON WITH A MADMAN

Who has woe? Who has sorrow? Who has strife? Who has complaints? Who has needless bruises? Who has bloodshot eyes? Those who linger over wine, who go to sample bowls of mixed wine. Do not gaze at wine when it is red, when it sparkles in the cup, when it goes down smoothly! In the end it bites like a snake and poisons like a viper. Proverbs 23: 29-32

You can't reason with a madman! An alcoholic is literally insane. Let me explain.

You will find, as the disease of alcoholism progresses, your drinker is not the man you once new and loved. His personality is continuously undergoing changes. He becomes irrational, undependable, dishonest, immoral, immature, and selfish. He's easily distracted, agitated, and angered. His rationale doesn't make sense to anyone but himself. Conversations spiral in circles.

On the surface he may look and sound normal; so, you reason you should be able to communicate with him logically and rationally, but this is not the case. The chemical deterioration of the prefrontal cortex, which is the moral seat of the brain, has made it difficult it for him to separate between right and wrong. You watch as he tries to force pieces of information to fit together in his brain, but he can no longer make the connections between actions and consequences.

His morality, focus, and logic weaken even more when he is drunk.

I remember when my husband would come stumbling into our home after a night out drinking with his buddies. His speech would be slurred. He was sloppy drunk. He followed me around the house trying to make conversation — often asking me the same question every five minutes. I'd look at him in disbelief and say, "Okay, listen closely. You already asked me that question three times, but here's the answer again..." Give him a few more minutes, and he asked the same question again. He honestly couldn't remember my answer, or even that he had already asked me that question in the first place.

The chemical toxins have taken their toll — causing the alcoholic's brain to shrink. There are fewer electrical impulses. His reactions are sluggish and confused. He is impulsive and selfish. He can no longer discern the difference between right and wrong.

My husband used to be a good Christian man. He was an ordained deacon and church leader. He would take up the offering, have prayer, teach the Bible lesson before church, and greet the visitors. He used to attend church every weekend and go to prayer meetings on Wednesday nights. He was the first to sign up for a church work bee. Sadly, when he began drinking again, his personality began changing, too.

He asked for his name to be removed from the church books. He told dirty jokes, watched filthy TV shows, and made disgusting remarks to the check out ladies in the grocery line. He openly flirted with waitresses and our friends' wives in front of me. I was mortified. I was afraid to go anywhere with him, because you never knew what kind of filthy remarks would spill from his lips. Who was this guy?!

These types of behaviors are common with a chemically dependent person. The brain can no longer use simple judgment or forethought before acting out. He cannot connect his actions with consequences; therefore, his actions will become more and more irrational and embarrassing to be around.

One of the amazing things about alcoholism is that it is a progressive disease. It doesn't stop progressing even after the alcoholic quits drinking. Even if he begins to drink after years of being dry, the disease will have advanced to a stage as if he had never quit.

Wow, that's scary.

So, don't believe it when your drinker says he can learn to control his liquor, drink less, or have "just a few." It can't and won't happen. He may be able to "white knuckle it" for a time and become a "dry drunk," but he will eventually fall back into the old routine and progression of the disease,

2 You Can't Reason with a Madman

unless he is actively working a program of recovery, such as AA's 12-step program. That is just the nature of the disease. It is what it is...

Something else incredible is that the alcoholic's brain ceases to mature when he begins drinking. Growth stops. It is stuck at the age of when he first became an alcoholic; which in most cases is in his early teens. This is one of the reasons most alcoholics are so selfish and self-centered. They are still thinking like a teenager.

My husband is a perfectionist — when it comes to other people. He is quick to point out another's mistakes, even though his mistakes may be glaringly worse.

He is number one and expects the world to revolve around him. If this doesn't happen, he completely loses it and makes the whole family miserable with his ranting and raving.

I firmly believe, there is a huge battle raging between good and evil for the soul of my husband. If you are not following what you know to be right, you are not following God. Plain and simple. It's one way or the other — Christ or Satan. Choose one, but you can't choose both. For this reason our prayers should be doubled for the one we love.

I know my husband clung to his Bible when he was really drunk — searching for relief from heavy guilt and remorse. I can only imagine what horrifying darkness and despair Satan's evil forces surrounded him with. He was desperate for some ray of hope from his dismal existence. Reading his Bible gave him some relief.

Alcoholism is the result of genetics, choices he makes, and changes that have taken place in the brain due to continued exposure of toxins.

However, even though the disease of alcoholism is inherited, it is no excuse for the behavior involved with this disease. An alcoholic has an obligation to God to take care of his family and to live in accordance with God's laws — regardless. No excuses.

In retrospect, the challenge of sobriety awaiting our alcoholic can be daunting. How can he expect to change when he has so much cleaning up to do? You can rest assured that he will not wake up one sunny morning and decide to get sober. Nope. That is not going to happen.

There is a battle going on for your drinker's soul. Let us pray for our loved one's delivery from this horrible disease. God will be with us every step of the way.

Part 1: Understanding the Alcoholic

That's good news, because this is going to be a long, hard battle.

Describe your drinker's personality before he began drinking. Be specific.

Describe your drinker's personality after he began drinking. Be specific.

2 You Can't Reason with a Madman

The alcoholic's brain is incapable of grasping that bad things happen to him as a result of his actions. With this concept in mind, how can you get across to your drinker that what he is doing is detrimental to him and his loved ones?

IMPORTANT NOTE: Whatever it is you just wrote, don't try to implement your plan with your alcoholic. It may not be the right course to take. We will get more into the right approach later. At this point, you are just brainstorming an average person's reaction to an alcoholic's behavior.

3 ANGER FUELS ALCOHOLISM

Don't have anything to do with foolish and stupid arguments, because you know they produce quarrels. And the Lord's servant must not quarrel; instead, he must be kind to everyone, able to teach, not resentful. Those who oppose him he must gently instruct, in the hope that God will grant them repentance leading them to a knowledge of the truth, and that they will come to their senses and escape from the trap of the devil, who has taken them captive to do his will. 2 Timothy 2: 23-26

Anger and violence are common behaviors for an alcoholic. One of the reasons for this behavior is because feels he needs an excuse to drink. The way he sees it, the easiest way to get this "excuse" is to get someone angry with him by pushing her buttons. I have experienced this phenomenon on numerous occasions.

Here's an example of how my husband bombards me with a barrage of accusations and argumentative statements. (During these tirades, I try hard not to get angry and not to be self-righteous about it — keeping in mind his mind is not operating correctly.)

One sunny summer afternoon, the birds were singing, and the butterflies were floating past my dining room window. I was sitting at the table working on income taxes, when my husband swaggers in. He'd been drinking, as usual, but wasn't sloppy drunk. He made his way straight to where I was working, glared down at me and angrily began his tirade.

"You need a plan for getting your weight under control," he blurted out.

"Yeah, I suppose so." (Not my usual reaction when discussing my weight.)

3 Anger Fuels Alcoholism

"How come it's taking you so long to get these taxes done?!"

"I've been pretty busy."

"I hope you know where you put all the receipts."

"I think so."

"Did you remember to get dog food? Did you get the right kind this time?"

"Yes."

"Where's supper? You never can make supper on time!"

"It's four o'clock. I haven't started it yet."

"You always wait until the last minute. Why can't you make a decent meal ahead of time instead of waiting until the last minute?"

I didn't say anything. I just got up and began preparing dinner.

It's amazing how quickly an alcoholic can change the topic when he fails to get the instant angry response that his disease craves. He can switch his train of thought at lightning speeds. Remember, the disease is cunning, reckless and conniving.

Fortunately, that day I had been ready for him, and I wasn't angry – amused maybe, but not angry. After all, it is quite a feat to change the topic in such rapid-fire succession. I knew that I shouldn't take him too seriously. This wasn't my husband talking. It was the bottle. The real purpose behind the attacks was to get me angry; so he'd feel vindicated for drinking. I knew I didn't need to take his accusations personally.

Detaching from these types of situations is necessary for our sanity, and in order for us to do that, we need a divine intervention on our behalf. Here is where our need for the Spirit's presence in our lives is so essential.

Every morning I commit myself to God. I ask him to open my eyes to the real situation and give me gentleness, patience and understanding for the day ahead. I could never be that way in my own strength. Oh, no... And when the Lord grants me that kind of peace, I am able to stand against Satan's wiles, and not be ruffled by the erratic statements of my alcoholic.

It is interesting to watch how, when the alcoholic can't get someone angry with him, the anger turns and rolls back onto him. He looks around, confused. He's not sure what to do next. He now has no excuse to drink. His plan has failed. This is good. Your indifference, or detachment, in volatile situations will expedite his recovery. It will cause him to realize he *needs* that drink, whether you are angry with him or not.

Part 1: Understanding the Alcoholic

He will come to realize that he drinks when he's happy, to celebrate, when he's angry, to get even, when he's sad, to numb the pain, when he's worried, to forget his problems, and to unwind, to relax, which pretty much means all the time.

Without your participation in getting angry over his antics, you are helping him discover that the disease is the enemy, not you.

As a side note, there will be times when you find yourself giving into frustration, resentment, and anger. It happens to the best of us. We're human, and sometimes the craziness of it all will get to be just too much for you. You will blow up. It happens.

If it does, don't become discouraged. Just get up, brush the dust off your knees, and move on. Pray for God's forgiveness, patience, and understanding. He hears your prayers, and he promises he will answer, if you will seek Him with all your heart.

Ask and it will be given to you; seek and you will find; knock and the door will be opened to you. For everyone who asks receives; he who seeks finds; and to him who knocks, the door will be opened. Matthew 7:6-9

Write about a time your alcoholic got angry with you. Include the conversation he had with you during his angry outburst.

What was your reaction to your alcoholic's anger?

3 Anger Fuels Alcoholism

What were the results of how you handled the situation?

Do you think the outcome would have been different, if you had handled it differently? Why or why not?

Write a quick prayer you could use, when you are confronted with an angry alcoholic.

4 THE DOG, THE GOLDFISH, OR WHATEVER

It is to one's honor to avoid strife, but every fool is quick to quarrel. Proverbs 20:3

I know we have already covered the need for the alcoholic to create a confrontational situation in order to get the excuse he needs to go drink, but I feel compelled to write a chapter about THE DOG... Actually, depending on your situation, it might be the dog, the goldfish, or whatever else he may find to push your buttons. You fill in the blank...

At first, I thought I was the only one who suffered from playing second fiddle to the dog, but in retrospect, after talking to other women and men living with an alcoholic, I found out that this phenomenon is a common occurrence; therefore, I decided to devote an entire chapter specifically on this topic.

When my husband would come home, our dog, Pookie, a little pug mix, would meet him at the door. Her entire little body would vibrate with happiness. She didn't care if he were drunk, high, stinky, clean, angry, or happy. I would meet him, too. Only thing was, I'd be totally ignored, while the dog would get, "Oh, how's my sweet little baby..." Gush... Gush... Gush... He'd then reach down and scratch her lovingly on the head while staring endearingly into her soft brown eyes. I'd hardly get a second glance, he'd push me aside, and then he'd stalk into the living room, grab the remote, plop down onto his ratty brown recliner, and flick on the news.

I felt so dejected! To top it all off, the dog would hop up onto his lap, and they'd kiss and hug and snuggle. He would whisper sweet nothings into her ear, while hollering at me to come look how cute she was. The whole scene made me sick to my stomach. I would cry silently and long for those words, hugs, and kisses to be directed at me, but alas — it was not to

4 The Dog, The Goldfish, or Whatever

be. My husband knew that he was hurting me. We had discussed it on several occasions. Yet, he continued to do it anyway.

I finally came to the realization, that this was typical behavior for an alcoholic. An alcoholic will make it his business to study into and specialize in whatever it takes to push your buttons. He desperately needs to get someone angry with him – again, for that excuse to drink. That's how the he thinks.

"If I can get my wife angry with me, I have a good excuse to go out and have a few with the boys. Who could blame me -- living with a whiney old nag like that! She's soooo sensitive! Give me a break! I deserve a little time to relax away from that *@#!$%* woman!"

And he goes storming off to the nearest bar to spend some quality time with his drinking buddies.

Well, his motive finally became clear to me, and that's when my perspective began to change. My anger began to melt away, and I began to feel sorry for him. I now see him as a poor old drunk who only has a dog to love on.

I don't feel sorry for myself anymore. I feel sorry for him.

I no longer pay any attention to him when he showers his love on Pookie. I just think to myself, "Well, I'm glad he feels loving toward something," and I let it go at that.

Here's the clincher – as soon as he saw that what he was doing no longer hurt me, he quit paying attention to the dog. Now, when he comes in the door he totally ignores her, too. When she tries to jump in his lap, he pushes her off without a second thought. Pookie has been dethroned.

Ha! Who would have thought? Go figure!

What are some things your drinker does to push your buttons?

Part 1: Understanding the Alcoholic

What are your usual responses to his actions?

Why do you think you have these responses?

Remembering that an angry response just feeds his alcoholic needs, what would be a better way to handle this type of situation?

4 The Dog, The Goldfish, or Whatever

What do you think will be his response to your new ways of handling volatile situations?

Try your new response and record your alcoholic's new reaction.

5 FINANCIAL RUIN

Give to everyone what you owe them: If you owe taxes, pay taxes; if revenue, then revenue; if respect, then respect; if honor, then honor. Romans 13:7

As sure as the sun rises in the East and sets in the West, the alcoholic will experience financial ruin if he does not get sober. It is inevitable; unless, there is an enabler feeding him money, which is a bad thing, because it will just prolong the disease.

Case in point… My husband and I enjoyed being the proud owners of a very high credit score for decades into our marriage. It was consistently in the 800s. We wouldn't flinch when a lender would tell us, "We need to pull up your credit scores." My husband and I would absentmindedly chuckle to ourselves and smugly smile at one another. Then we'd begin tapping our fingers on the arms of our chairs as we stared at the ceiling in boredom waiting for them to come back all smiles practically begging us to give them our business — with bottom low interest rates — as we knew they would. Those were the good old days.

It wasn't that we were rich either! We were poor by most respects with an income of around $40,000 a year between us. It was just that my husband was a money guru, who was very conscientious about paying bills on time, investing wisely, not creating any unnecessary debt, paying off debt ahead of time, and budgeting our money carefully. Early on in our marriage, I was very happy to give him the reigns of our money, as he was way better than I was at saving and managing the finances. I trusted his judgment impeccably.

But along came alcohol and drugs.

5 Financial Ruin

At first the signs were vague and inconspicuous. A late bill here, a forgotten bill on the floor of the truck there.

Then, my husband's job began to be affected by his drinking.

One day it would be, "I'm not doing much right now anyway. I think I'll stay home today."

"It looks like it might rain," on another.

Or maybe the classic, "It's too cold," or "It's too hot."

"I don't feel very well this morning. I think I might be coming down with something. I'd better take it easy today." Ever hear that one? The reality being that he was too hung over to go to work

Then, he began coming home later and later. He always had some sob story about how terrible people were at work, or how things broke down and slowed him up. He just had "a few beers" for "medicinal purposes" to help him unwind. What was wrong with that?

"Get off my back!" he'd say.

Down, down, down the drain went our finances.

As liquor took over my husband's life, our family financial situation began to look more and more grim. My husband's income over the last few years has gradually trickled down to the negative mark on our taxes, and my $40,000/year salary just couldn't cover all of the expenses.

Today, we regularly get phone calls from bill collectors. I tremble and quake at the very thought of anyone pulling up our credit score. Bills aren't paid until the last minute, if at all. Grace periods are our friends. Loans and credit payments are paid at the minimum required. Credit cards are always maxed out. Creditors reject our applications for more credit or loans. I know my husband owes a lot of people money for personal loans he's made behind my back. (I don't know how many people or how much.)

There just isn't as much money to go around. Bottom line, we owe more people money and are making less. The picture does not look good.

As my husband's financial contribution to the family became smaller and smaller, so did the numbers in my checkbook. Who was I kidding? I couldn't keep this up. We were going down — fast.

I was a nervous wreck, trying to do for our family what two people had been doing together for twenty years. I was attempting to clean up his mess. I was trying to cover his responsibilities. This couldn't be a good thing. I began to question the sanity of what I was doing.

Fortunately, I soon became aware of the absurdity of this whole Superwoman thing. My slowly taking over what should have been my husband's responsibilities was actually enabling him to continue his reckless behavior. The more I rescued him from the consequences of his behavior the sicker he became.

In time I began to see that in order to give my husband a fighting chance at sobriety, I would have to let go of our financial security for the time being. If our credit score needed to crash, so be it...

I no longer trust my husband with our money. I would no longer try to handle all the finances by myself. I would no longer try to pay all the bills.

We now have separate checking accounts. I am paying out the bare minimum of our bills to keep a roof over our heads and food in the children's mouths. I am unable to continue making the payments for any of our investments, his truck, his insurance, or to donate towards any of his endeavors. If am finding divides developing in not only our finances, but also in other areas of our marriage. The chasms are widening.

So, as of now, we are barely squeaking out an existence on my salary. We are in survival mode, but gratefully, I can honestly say, "God is providing. Praise Him..."

How have your finances been affected by being in a relationship with an alcoholic?

5 Financial Ruin

Is your family's money being used for things for which God would approve? If not, name the expenses, which need to go?

How can wasteful spending be stopped? If so, how? Be specific.

Part 1: Understanding the Alcoholic

Do you need to find a way to increase your income? If so, what type of a plan can you come up with to make this happen?

Important Note: Do not be confrontational with your drinker when it comes to money. There will come a time when you will need to evaluate whether you are enabling the drinking through your financial support. We will cover more on this later.

6 ADULTERY

Another thing you do: You flood the Lord's altar with tears. You weep and wail because he no longer pays attention to your offerings or accepts them with pleasure from your hands. You ask, "Why?" It is because the Lord is acting as the witness between you and the wife of your youth, because you have broken faith with her, though she is your partner, the wife of your marriage covenant. Has not the Lord made them one? In flesh and spirit they are his. And why one? Because he was seeking godly offspring. So guard yourself in your spirit, and do not break faith with the wife of your youth. "I hate divorce," says the Lord God of Israel, "and I hate a man's covering himself with violence as well as with his garment," says the Lord Almighty. So guard yourself in your spirit, and do not break faith. Malachi 2: 13-16

This is a very painful chapter for me to write. There is nothing that tears at my heart more than adultery (except maybe death). The betrayal, pain of rejection, the total sense of loss, and loads of anger — no, make that uncontainable rage. Actually, it makes me cry even now just thinking about it. So, know this article is written from the heart and with a lot of tears on my keyboard.

When I first learned of my husband affair, I was devastated. No one can understand this kind of hurt unless they have experienced it. I imagine it is close to the same as losing a child. It is fall on the floor, wish you were dead, throw up and sob, curse God and the day you met your husband kind of pain. The kind of pain that rips your heart out and yet at the same time feels like ten thousand knives stabbing your stomach and twisting. I cried out loud, hit things, threw things, cursed, and yelled at him and God. I wished I were dead. It is a kind of emotion I had never experienced before. It was so deep and to the core. I now understood why people in the Bible would sit in ashes, rip their clothes, and shave their heads, when they fell into utter despair. I wanted to roll around in the ashes and shrivel up to nothing. It was an intense experience. It lasted a couple of days. That's the best way I can describe it.

I don't understand this kind of excruciating pain. I guess that's why Jesus said, the only reason for divorce is adultery. He knew the agonizing pain it brings to the betrayed spouse. He knew that this is the hardest thing known to mankind to forgive – a tearing asunder of two that were joined as one – kind of like the atom bomb. It was never meant to be. He also knew of the problems it could cause to all those involved — especially the children. Oh, the dear children.

There are so many questions swirling around in my mind — waiting to be answered. What about the other lover? Did she pass on diseases to my husband? Is she pregnant? Is she still in contact with my husband? Is he still seeing or calling her? What kind of relationship did they have? Are they still emotionally attached? How long has this really been going on? Did he spend our money on her? Can I ever trust him again? Do I want to? All of these questions are going to have to be answered to your satisfaction, before you can decide whether you want to continue in the relationship.

Some believe if an alcoholic has an affair, it is best not to tell the spouse about it, because it would cause too much pain. Also, don't tell who it is or any of the details, because it could bring up more things that would cause more pain now and in the future. I'm not so sure about this theory. It may have been better for my sanity, if I didn't know. After all, how much pain can a human endure anyway?

However, rest assured, God saw what happened, where they were, with whom, and how many times. The Holy Spirit begged my husband not to do it. He knows all the sordid details. He knew the chaos it would create. He wept when he witnessed his decision to deny His tugging at his heart not to break the seventh commandment – for nothing is secret to God.

Many times, the alcoholic daydreams to himself – how wonderful it would be to find someone else who would love him "unconditionally," and who would not only put up with his alcoholism, but drink with him.

"Wow, what a perfect woman she would be! She would understand me," he reasons.

6 Adultery

The reality of it is – that type of woman will NOT make him happy. They may think they are happy for a time, but it will not last with two sick minds trying to use each other for their own selfish gains.

Don't get all depressed that he has left you for someone else.

I'd say in 95% of the cases, the alcoholic would drop his dream girl and come staggering back to you. Just wait. It will happen. So, don't be all worried about that. Even if you don't want him back, he'll be back. He'll show up on your doorstep, like he never left and nothing ever happened. Oh, boy…

When I first found out my husband had an affair, my knee jerk reaction was to divorce immediately. In fact, I got in the car, went to the bank and took out the money for a retainer fee, and drove straight to the divorce lawyer's office. I started divorce proceedings the same day. In my mind, our marriage was over.

Of course, my family and friends were all shocked with the news and encouraged me to quickly go through with the divorce. However, as time passed, I began to study into this adultery/alcoholism thing. What I learned was that adultery and alcoholism are best bedfellows. They go hand in hand — no pun intended.

Remember, we talked in an earlier chapter about how the alcoholic brain does not function properly. The moral value system has shut down, and the alcoholic cannot discern right from wrong. Even though this is true, it does not excuse his behavior. He made the decision to make the ultimate sacrifice — the potential loss of his marriage. It was through a series of thought processes that he decided to bring this sin into fruition.

He is accountable to you, his family, and most of all to God for what he has done. There will be consequences. That is God's promise for He is a just God. Marriage is a boundary set by God and loyalty between two partners has been vowed. If the boundary of being faithful to your spouse is broken, the adulterer will have to answer to God…

God will not allow such a thing to go without notice. He turns his face from those who are involved with adultery. It is a grievous and evil thing. His holiness does not allow Him to be in the presence of those involved in it.

There is something you need to realize and hold close to your heart – you are not to blame. Sure, you may not have been the perfect wife or had the best reactions to what your alcoholic has dished out to you, but you need to realize — it was his choice. Period. End of story. Don't listen to any of his excuses. Just know the excuses are the disease talking. As usual, he is trying to put the blame on someone else — you. Don't fall for it.

After the affair is found out, you will need to decide whether you want to continue your marriage or not. Please, do not make a hasty decision as I did. Take time to discuss the circumstances with your pastor and Godly counsel, Bible study, and much prayer. You are no longer bound by your marriage vows to stay in this marriage. God has granted you a way out, but remember that divorce is not easy either. Whichever way you choose will involve a long journey of hurt, loneliness, healing, and forgiveness. If you do decide to try and save your marriage, there are some things upon which you must insist.

Your spouse will have to make amends with God, you, and your family. It will not be easy for him; neither should it be.

If your alcoholic is sober, there may be a possibility of salvaging your marriage, but the guilty spouse is going to have to be 100% transparent to you. He will have to gladly let you check the cell phone and its records, bank records, welcome you to drop in and check up on him during the day at work, listen to voice messages, etc.... If he is unwilling to do this, I would question the sincerity of your spouse. What is it he is still hiding? If he wants your relationship to be restored, he will have to make a lot of concessions, be happy to do it, and be so thankful that you are giving him a second chance at your marriage, that he will be willing to do anything to show you that you are there only one for him. These restorative measures are necessary for his recovery and yours.

If he is unwilling to be totally transparent, don't take him back. You are not valuable enough to him. He is still not being truthful with you. Don't listen to his accusations that you just don't trust him. That's pretty funny. How can he expect you to trust him? Pretty ironic, I'd say…

If your alcoholic is still actively drinking, you cannot count on his being honest. His brain just isn't there yet. Even though he may make a thousand promises of love and commitment, be aware that an alcoholic's promises are like ropes of sand. You will have to be very committed to being watchful and aware of what is really going on in his life.

6 Adultery

You may find it necessary to separate for your mental, physical and spiritual safety until he gets sober. After he gets sober, you can reassess the situation from a more sane perspective.

Forgiveness is a big word. Forgiving an unfaithful spouse is an extremely tall order that will have to come from God. You will need to seek it from Him. Go to God and open your heart to Him. He understands. He will hold you in His arms and listen quietly while you vent. He understands all about betrayal. After a while, a soft reassuring peace will waft over you and comfort you in your time of loss. The grieving process has begun. Forgiveness will come, but it will need to come from the Father. Receive His gift gladly.

If you refuse forgiveness, it will slowly eat you alive from the inside out. Don't hang on to resentment and anger in order to punish your mate. It will only destroy you — a slow, lingering death. Trust Him with all your heart and let Him comfort and guide your future. He will, if you but ask. Claim His promise:

"Though the mountains be shaken and the hills be removed, yet my unfailing love for you will not be shaken nor my covenant of peace be removed," says the Lord, who has compassion on you." Isaiah 54:9-11

I am *not* saying to forget. When there is sin, there are consequences. Trust is fragile, and when broken, will take time to heal. Be kind and patient with yourself. Don't force yourself to trust again anytime soon. Allow God and your husband time to heal your broken heart.

Being in the sisterhood of cheated-on wives, makes me have extreme empathy with other women suffering under this curse and trying to restore what is left of their lives. I pray that my experience and reflections may be of some benefit to someone going through the same hell as I did.

God help us all.

If you are married to your alcoholic, has he ever cheated on you?

Part 1: Understanding the Alcoholic

If he has, describe the circumstances and your feelings.

Do you wish to forgive your husband and stay in the marriage or end it?

What would it take for you to trust your spouse again? If he wants to stay in this relationship, let him know what your needs are.

How did the affair affect others in your family, such as your children?

6 Adultery

What needs to happen in order for your children to understand how adults should respect each other and act maturely to one another?

What are you prepared to do to teach your children what a mature relationship looks like?

PART 2: HELPING THE ALCOHOLIC

7 THE ALCOHOLIC'S CONFESSION

I do not understand what I do. For what I want to do I do not do, but what I hate I do. Romans 7:15

If an alcoholic were able to talk honestly about his feelings, here is what I believe he would say:

1. Don't try to control me for only the bottle has control of me. Trying to force me to church, get a job, or to quit drinking is a waste of your time.

2. Don't let me scare you. I know I am scary at times. I scream, yell, and hurt you and the children emotionally and physically. Don't allow me do it. Protect yourselves and our babies. I can't control myself. I need your help with protecting my family. Do whatever it takes to keep yourself and the children safe. I will rant and rave about it, but do it in spite of my objections and arguments. I need to be strong enough to do what is right over what I tell you to do.

3. Don't believe my lies. I will lie about where I have been, what I've been doing, and how many drinks I've had. "A few," can mean 24 cans of beer. Please don't fall for my lame excuses. Let me know you don't believe me. Tell me that you know I am lying, that you know the truth. I will respect you for it, even though I will become defensive and try to deny everything.

7 The Alcoholic's Confession

4. Don't believe any of my promises. I may be sincere when I make the promises, but my disease keeps me from carrying them out. Remember, actions speak louder than words. Pay attention to my behavior, not my words. Don't expect me to follow through my promises, because I won't.

5. Don't take over my responsibilities. When you take over my responsibilities, I lose what little respect for myself I have left. I will do my best to try and get you to fix my mistakes. I will try to con you, shame you, or guilt you into taking care of my responsibilities by acting pitiful or sick. Sometimes, I will get angry and try to force you into doing them. Please, don't allow me to manipulate you. Either let it not get done at all, or allow me to take care of my own responsibilities. This will actually help me out more than if you had taken care of my responsibility for me.

6. Get some help for you and the children. Go to Al-Anon, our pastor, a counselor, or anyone who understands alcoholics and knows how to help our family. I know I am hard to live with, but my sickness keeps me angry with myself. I have lost control of myself; therefore, I will cling to my control of you and the children. I will become terrified at the thought of losing you, because I depend on you to keep me out of trouble. I will hate your looking for help. I will fight it. I will feel you slipping out of my tightly grasped fist. I will not be happy about your finding help, but you must – for the sake of the family.

7. Don't allow me to scare you, abuse you, or hurt you or the children. My illness may cause me to do some out-of-my-head crazy things sometimes. When I begin acting like that, get in the car and drive away to a safe place away from me. If I am angry all the time and abusive, we may need to separate. Please, don't tell me where you are or when you are leaving. I will go ballistic, and I will follow you, and the abuse will continue. I am so sorry. This is not me. I need to get help before we can be together.

Part 2: Helping the Alcoholic

8. Pray for me. I am unable to pray for myself. Please lift me up to our Creator several times throughout the day. I need your prayers.

9. Send help. The only kind of help that I will listen to is the help from an ex-drunk, or someone that is a specialist in alcoholic behavior — someone that understands what I am going through, or has escaped this insidious grasp that alcohol holds around his neck himself. I will listen to what he has to say, but I may not be ready to quit when he talks to me. I may kick him out of the house, but whatever words he says will be like fresh rain droplets of hope upon my parched soul. I will remember his words and store them in my heart for whenever I am ready to become sober.

10. I long for what you have — the peace of not having to run after the next drink all day and all night. I dream of having a clear conscience. I would sleep like a baby and not have a care in the world. Oh, how I wish for peace like that in my soul.

11. I am sorry for what I have done to this family. I carry the heavy burden of guilt on my shoulders, for I know what I am doing to you and the family. I wish I could stop, but it is too difficult; so, I continue to drink away the guilt. It is easier that way.

12. I miss the way things used to be when I didn't drink. That seems like such a long time ago. I am so sick. I cannot ever see us being a happy family again. I need my booze to heal the pain. I cannot give it up for anything or anyone. I need the medication.

13. I love you. I know this is the hardest thing for you to believe, but I do. I love you, the children, and the family. You are all I have. It scares me to lose you. Where would I be without you?

I believe this is what an alcoholic would say, if his mind were clear enough to honestly speak the truth.

7 The Alcoholic's Confession

What surprised you the most about what you just read and why?

Now that you better understand what your alcoholic is really thinking, what changes would you like to be strong enough to make?

8 INTERCESSORY PRAYERS

And the prayer offered in faith will make the sick person well; the Lord will raise him up. If he has sinned, he will be forgiven. Therefore confess your sins to each other and pray for each other so that you may be healed. The prayer of a righteous man is powerful and effective. James 5:15-20

Sometimes, we feel like we failed to do everything in our power to protect our alcoholic from falling into addiction. Other times, we are made to feel it is our fault that we have driven him to the bottle. Granted, we are not perfect and have made some mistakes, we should never feel that this disease is our fault. It is not. Keep in mind it is a disease brought on by the alcoholic's poor choices, genetic makeup, and by Satan's devious plan for the drinker's downfall.

Every created being has been endowed with the gift of choice. However, Satan is a master at carefully planning the series of events within a person's life to gradually lead the unsuspecting victim into situations in which choices between good and evil will have to be made. He comes to an impasse — to drink or not to drink.

Time and time again, the Holy Spirit pleads for repentance, but the mind-numbing effects of alcohol soon quiet His gentle heart-whispers. The power of choice is gone. He can no longer stop in his own power. He is trapped in the disease of alcoholism. There is only one way out — through the power given to us through our heavenly Father. To receive this power he must learn to pray effectively.

Prayer, a supernatural war tactic, is a powerful resource Christians have the privilege and duty of using. It is something we can do for the alcoholic.

8 Intercessory Prayer

You may feel that your prayers are useless, because your alcoholic has rebelled against the pleadings of the Holy Spirit. You may feel that once a person has made the choice and continues to demonstrate a negative attitude towards Christ and all things righteous, that there is no hope for his soul. He's made his choice, and that's all there is to it.

Let me assure you that this presumption is absolutely false. God uses his believers to be witnesses and intercessors to the throne of God on the alcoholic's behalf. Today, Christians are called to offer intercessory prayers for the fallen, just the same as they were in the Bible.

So then, how exactly do we go about this business of offering up intercessory prayers on behalf of our loved one?

First of all, having the Holy Spirit in your heart is essential. In order to align yourself with the work of the Holy Spirit, your heart needs to be in one accord with His objectives and motives. If he is not in your heart, your prayer will be ineffective, and you might as well not waste your time.

The Lord is far from the wicked but he hears the prayer of the righteous. Proverbs 15: 29

So, how do you know if the Spirit is in you? Ask yourself, "Are the fruits of the spirit apparent in my personal and business life?" Be honest with yourself. Pray for God to reveal to you areas in your life that are not in accordance with His Word and purpose. Prayerfully, consider the verses below.

The acts of the sinful nature are obvious: sexual immorality, impurity and debauchery; idolatry and witchcraft; hatred, discord, jealousy, fits of rage, selfish ambition, dissensions, factions and envy; drunkenness, orgies, and the like. I warn you, as I did before, that those who live like this will not inherit the kingdom of God. But the fruit of the Spirit is love, joy, peace, patience, kindness, goodness, faithfulness, gentleness and self-control. Against such things there is no law. Galatians 5: 19-23

So, how do you measure up by these standards?

If you have secret sins you are holding onto, or people you have wronged and not made it right with them, your prayers will be of no effect.

Part 2: Helping the Alcoholic

Be open and honest with God. He knows your heart. He has seen all that you have done. If you don't want to give up your sin, tell him. Ask him to remove the desire to continue to sin from your heart. He will.

If you have hurt someone, go to them and ask forgiveness. Hold no resentments towards others. Ask God to give you a forgiving spirit towards others' mistakes.

Next, go to God with a contrite heart and ask Him to forgive you for your sins. Believe that you are forgiven. He has promised to forgive if we ask.

"Come now, let us reason together," says the Lord. "Though your sins are like scarlet, they shall be as white as snow; though they are red as crimson, they shall be like wool." Isaiah 1: 18

When you give your sins to God and open your life to the Holy Spirit's leadings, you are ready to pray for your alcoholic. Your motives and goals have become one with our Savior, and you are at the place where He can work through you.

I will give you a new heart and put a new spirit in you; I will remove from you your heart of stone and give you a heart of flesh. Ezekiel 36:26

Once your heart is made new, the first thing you will want to pray for is the forgiveness of our alcoholic. His inebriated brain is toxic and has become incapable of rationale decisions; therefore, it is your duty as a Christian to intercede on his behalf. Amazing as it sounds, we can ask for the forgiveness of others, and God will answer. Here are some Biblical examples of instances where this happened...

Moses prayed for the forgiveness of the children of Israel.

[Moses talking] *"In accordance with your great love, forgive the sin of these people, just as you have pardoned them from the time they left Egypt until now."* The Lord replied, *"I have forgiven them, as you asked." Numbers 14: 19, 20*

Jesus prayed for the forgiveness for those who crucified him.

8 Intercessory Prayer

Jesus said, *"Father, forgive them, for they do not know what they are doing..."* Luke 23:24

Next, pray that the atoning blood of Christ may be demonstrated in your drinker's life by surrounding him daily with the light and peace of the Holy Spirit's presence. Pray for the Spirit to continuously speak to your alcoholic's heart — to guide him to do what is right.

Keep in mind that your loved one still has the opportunity to make whichever choices he wants; however, he will continuously have the Spirit speaking to him, guiding him. He is no longer alone with the devil in his decision making process. God is waiting and ready for his turn from evil. He will guide him and do all in His power to lead him to the right decisions.

There are some places your alcoholic will go that the angels will not enter. But because of your prayers and the love of our Father, which is in Heaven, the Holy Spirit will enter these places and will still speak to the alcoholic.

Where can I go from your Spirit? Where can I flee from your presence? If I go up to the heavens, you are there; if I make my bed in the depths, you are there. Psalm 139:7, 8

The next thing to pray for is that God will arrange the events in your alcoholic's life to open his eyes to the reality of Satan's lies. He needs to realize that he is not really happy with the way things are going in his life.

His eyes are on the ways of men; he sees their every step. There is no dark place, no deep shadow, where evildoers can hide. Job 34:21, 22

God can make things happen in his life that show him the grievous nature of his sins. We don't know what needs to happen. We may think we know what needs to happen, but we really don't. Only God knows the alcoholic's heart and circumstances that brought him to the place where he is now. Only Christ can know what needs to happen in his life to show him his errors. Trust in Him to do His work, and stay out of His way.

Trust in the LORD with all your heart and lean not on your own understanding; in all your ways acknowledge him, and he will make your paths straight.

Proverbs 3: 5, 6

The last thing I would suggest is to persevere in your prayers. This may be the hardest thing you ever do. Answers to your prayer may happen rapidly. You may start to see results in hours, but be prepared for your prayers to take years to answer. Don't give up! God will give you strength to pray on.

Then Jesus told his disciples a parable to show them that they should always pray and not give up. Luke 18:1

Who have you offended that you need to make amends with?

When would be a good time to do this?

8 Intercessory Prayer

What sins need cleaning in your own life?

Ask the Lord to take these sins from you. Then, write an intercessory prayer for your alcoholic.

Part 2: Helping the Alcoholic

9 PRAYING FOR HEALING

So keep up your courage, men, for I have faith in God that it will happen just as he told me. Acts 27:25

As the wife of an alcoholic, I have often wondered, since alcoholism is a disease, wouldn't Jesus have healed my husband, if he were living in Jesus' time? Better yet, couldn't he heal him now, if I prayed the right prayer in the right way? Couldn't I be like the friends of the paralytic who let down him down through the roof on a sheet in front of Jesus to be healed? Then Jesus could heal him. I've actually imagined myself doing this.

I know Jesus can heal my husband, if he but thinks the thought or breathes the words, "You are healed." And if He can do this, why doesn't he. I've prayed for my husband's healing for so long, surely he's heard my prayers by now. So, why hasn't he healed him?!

I think I have finally found my answer in the following Bible story, found in the book of John, chapter 5, starting with verse one.

Some time later, Jesus went up to Jerusalem for one of the Jewish festivals. Now there is in Jerusalem near the Sheep Gate a pool, which in Aramaic is called Bethesda and which is surrounded by five covered colonnades. Here a great number of disabled people used to lie—the blind, the lame, the paralyzed. One who was there had been an invalid for thirty-eight years. When Jesus saw him lying there and learned that he had been in this condition for a long time, he asked him, "Do you want to get well?"

"Sir," the invalid replied, "I have no one to help me into the pool when the water is stirred. While I am trying to get in, someone else goes down ahead of me."

9 Praying for Healing

> *Then Jesus said to him, "Get up! Pick up your mat and walk." At once the man was cured; he picked up his mat and walked.*
>
> *The day on which this took place was a Sabbath, and so the Jewish leaders said to the man who had been healed, "It is the Sabbath; the law forbids you to carry your mat."*
>
> *But he replied, "The man who made me well said to me, 'Pick up your mat and walk.'"*
>
> *So they asked him, "Who is this fellow who told you to pick it up and walk?"*
>
> *The man who was healed had no idea who it was, for Jesus had slipped away into the crowd that was there.*
>
> *Later Jesus found him at the temple and said to him, "See, you are well again. Stop sinning or something worse may happen to you." The man went away and told the Jewish leaders that it was Jesus who had made him well. John 5:1-15*

It seems to me that this story lays out the conditions for healing in a straightforward way. Let's take a closer look at these steps to recovery.

1. Jesus went to him. The sick person was too sick to come to him, but deep down he saw his need for a savior, a healer. This was shown in that he was at the pool in the first place. He was humbly and patiently waiting for someone to put him in the waters when they were stirred. Maybe, this is would be shown in the alcoholic by his going to AA or detox. He is putting himself in a place where he feels someone can help him be healed.

2. The invalid wanted to get well. This point is so very important. Jesus asked him point blank, "Do you want to get well?" If he had said, "No," Jesus would have moved on. He is not going to heal someone that doesn't want to be healed. In the same way, your alcoholic is going to have to get to the point where he wants healing and is willing to humbly go to the place of healing, before The Great Healer can work.

3. Jesus told the sick man to do something. The invalid had to take action in order for him to be healed. Jesus told the man, "Get up. Pick up your mat and walk!" The man could have ignored this command to action. He could have said, "I can't." And the healing process would have ended right then, but he didn't. He did what God told him to do. In the alcoholic's case, the command may be, "Go to rehab." It may be, "Stay away from

Part 2: Helping the Alcoholic

your alcoholic friends." It may be, "Quit your job," and so forth. You get the idea. Regardless of the action the Spirit directs the alcoholic in, it is necessary for him to follow His commands without question in order to get well. This is going to require commitment, humiliation, and faith on his part.

4. The last main point is that once he was healed, he could no longer go back to his old way of life. We read, "Later Jesus found him at the temple and said to him, 'See, you are well again. Stop sinning or something worse may happen to you.'" The healed man was not at liberty to resume his old life of sin after his encounter with his Savior. If he did, he was warned that things would end up worse than ever for him. Neither, can an alcoholic go about his business as usual. Things have to change. All things are new for him.

When he gives his life over to Jesus, he becomes a new creature. He has to develop different ways of handling hard situations. He needs to make new friends, stop hanging around the same place where he got into trouble. He is a new man in Christ – old things are "passed away."

I feel this story is a good example of God's healing process. If the steps are followed, the alcoholic will be healed — plain and simple.

So, this is what we can pray for. We can pray for God to come near our alcoholic and to stay near him. We can pray for Holy Spirit to whisper in his ear soothing offers of healing. We can pray for circumstances surrounding him to be conducive to his surrendering. These are things we can do, but the rest is up to our alcoholic. It is between him and God.

Don't ever give up the fight. As long as our alcoholic is breathing, keep on praying for him. This is all we can do; for even God can do nothing until the alcoholic takes the first step to healing — wanting to be healed.

Write a specific prayer of faith for your alcoholic to be put into a situation conducive to his humbly seeking God's healing.

9 Praying for Healing

10 MORE ON PRAYER

If my people, who are called by my name, will humble themselves and pray and seek my face and turn from their wicked ways, then will I hear from heaven and will forgive their sin and will heal their land. Now my eyes will be open and my ears attentive to the prayers offered in this place. 2 Chronicles 7:14,15

How should I pray for my husband? This was something I struggled with understanding for a long time. We've talked about intercessory prayer and praying for his healing, but how do you go about doing that? I pondered the questions: Is there some secret code for getting through to God? Is there a sequence of steps you need to take to be heard? What was I doing right? What was I doing wrong? How do I get some one-on-one time in the presence of God? How can I be assured that He hears and will answer?

Learning to pray for my husband became my passion. I searched the scriptures, prayed for guidance, listened to sermons, and read a number of books on the topic. In so doing, I have come to a number of conclusions. Here is a list of my great discoveries.

1. As discussed in the previous chapter, the first thing we need to do is get right with God. The Bible plainly states that unless we are right with our creator, our prayers will not go past the ceiling. So don't waste your time if you know you are knowingly sinning and are still unwilling want to stop.

I'm not saying you have to be perfect. No one is. But if you are doing something you know God doesn't want you to, and you make no effort to quit, He will not hear your prayers. I didn't say that. He said that. So, your

10 More on Prayer

first step will be to search your heart for any unrepentant sin and ask for forgiveness.

Therefore, my friends, I want you to know that through Jesus the forgiveness of sins is proclaimed to you." Acts 13:38

2. You must trust that God hears you, even though you may not see any sign of your prayers being answered right away. Don't give up!

"... Because they cried out to Him during the battle. He answered their prayers, because they trusted in Him... because the battle was God's..." 1 Chronicles 5:20, 22

So, there you have it. Just because you don't see the results of your prayers right away, don't give up. God is at work. Keep on praying. It may take years to see the results. In fact you may not know the affect of your prayers until you're in heaven, but rest assured, they are still being heard and answered with either a yes, no, or wait.

3. I can pray for the stumbling blocks in your loved-one's life to be removed.

God has given everyone the gift of choice. Choices began in the Garden of Eden. He put the "tree of good and evil" in the garden as a test of Adam and Eve's loyalty to Him. They failed the test, but they had the choice. I am sure all of heaven wept on that dark day of earth's history.

Our alcoholic has the same choice. "To drink or not to drink?" That is the question.

God will not force him get sober — no matter how much we pray. I have to accept that fact, but I can still pray for things to sway in his favor. I can pray for the bad influences in his life to be removed. I can pray for his relationships to be severed with his drinking buddies, that extenuating circumstances be tightened around him to push him in the direction of recovery.

When any Israelite or any alien living in Israel separates himself from me and sets up idols [alcohol] in his heart and puts a wicked stumbling block [anything that makes it easier for him to drink] before his face and then goes to a prophet to inquire of me, I the

Part 2: Helping the Alcoholic

Lord will answer him myself. I will set my face against that man and make him an example and a byword. I will cut him off from my people. Then you will know that I am the Lord. Ezekiel 14:7, 8 (Brackets and comments were added.)

4. I can pray that he will recognize the love of God for what it is.

... But I know you. I know that you do not have the love of God in your hearts. John 5:42

For I am convinced that neither death nor life, neither angels nor demons, neither the present nor the future, nor any powers, neither height nor depth, nor anything else in all creation, will be able to separate us from the love of God that is in Christ Jesus our Lord. At one time we too were foolish, disobedient, deceived and enslaved by all kinds of passions [drinking] and pleasures. We lived in malice and envy, being hated and hating one another. Romans 8:38, 39 (Brackets and comments were added.)

Now, get ready, because here comes the best part.

But when the kindness and love of God our Savior appeared, He saved us, not because of righteous things we had done, but because of his mercy. He saved us through the washing of rebirth and renewal by the Holy Spirit, whom he poured out on us generously through Jesus Christ our Savior, so that, having been justified by his grace, we might become heirs having the hope of eternal life. Titus 3:4-7 (bold type added)

Aaaah, yes! This is when the change will happen — the rebirth and renewal by the Holy Spirit. How exciting is that?! We're not talking about a dry drunk here. (We'll discuss the difference between a "dry drunk" and being "sober" later.)

No siree! This is a new personality. He will be sober. A new person filled with the Holy Spirit. Wow. What a promise!

5. Perseverance is so important. Don't be discouraged if you don't see apparent results to your prayers right away. You may not see any results, but God is working.

Then Jesus told his disciples a parable to show them that they should always pray and not give up. Read what He says.

10 More on Prayer

In a certain town there was a judge who neither feared God nor cared about men. And there was a widow in that town who kept coming to him with the plea,

"Grant me justice against my adversary."

For some time he refused. But finally he said to himself, "Even though I don't fear God or care about men, yet because this widow keeps bothering me, I will see that she gets justice, so that she won't eventually wear me out with her coming!"

And the Lord said, "Listen to what the unjust judge says. And will not God bring about justice for his chosen ones, who cry out to him day and night? Will he keep putting them off? I tell you, he will see that they get justice, and quickly..." Luke 18:1-8

The truth is you may be the only one praying for your alcoholic. You may be his only hope; so please, never give up.

Make a list of specific things you can pray for your drinker. Remember, you cannot pray that God force him to quit drinking.

Part 2: Helping the Alcoholic

Pray for any circumstance that God's Spirit leads you to think of that may lead him to the decision to quit drinking. Write at least five circumstances.

Now, write a specific intercessory prayer you can pray for your alcoholic. (Prayers for you will come later.)

11 DO'S AND DON'TS

Jesus looked at them and said, "With man this is impossible, but not with God; all things are possible with God." Mark 10:27

Angry frustration. That is the best way I would describe my feelings about living with my alcoholic husband.

My daughters and I had a front row seat to Satan's twisted show of destruction. We witnessed my husband's health, wealth, and values wash down the drain. As a result, our family was falling apart; the foundation of our family structure was crumbling.

I felt a sense of urgency. Surely, there must be something crazy enough that I could do to rock his world into sanity again. I wanted to grab him by the scruff of his neck, shake him until his teeth rattled, and shout in his ear, "Wake up, you idiot! Don't you see what you're doing to our family?" All I knew was if something didn't change soon, divorce was immanent.

So, I pulled out all the stops. I was going to get this guy's attention. The way I had it figured, he would have no choice but to quit drinking, see the error of his ways, and return unto the Lord.

I did what any self-respecting wife of a drunk would do; I yelled, begged, cried, reasoned, threw his clothes out the front door, locked him out of the house, moved out (and back in), searched for his booze and dumped it out, and packed up the kids and drove around looking for him, when he didn't come home from work. At first my actions were so shocking, they seemed to get his attention. But after all my hard work, you know what that crazy man had the nerve to say to me?

Part 2: Helping the Alcoholic

"Of course I'm not going to come home, because you act all crazy on me. I'm only using beer as a medication to get me through this !@#$@ marriage!"

Yep. That's what he said. He ended up blaming me for his drinking. The only thing I had accomplished was to give him another excuse to drink. All of my Superwoman tactics had been for nothing. I was exhausted mentally and physically. Apparently, my plan had backfired. It made matters worse, not better.

Why hadn't my perfect plan for my husband's redemption worked? What was I doing wrong? I needed some answers. I had hit my "rock bottom." I knew I needed help or else I would be the one to go insane. So began my research into the world of alcoholism and addictions.

Since I apparently didn't have a clue on how to handle this situation, I went looking for help and found the help I needed. I found an excellent local counselor who specializes in alcoholism within families, a therapy group specifically designed for addictions, Al-Anon meetings, a 12-step sponsor, open AA meetings, my pastor, friends, family, and God.

Attending all those meetings taught me that all that stuff that I had been doing just fueled the fires of alcoholism — not cure it. Boy, had I been wrong.

An alcoholic will not work to get sober until he is good and ready. All the fires of hell can be brought down upon him, but this will not make the slightest difference to him. Only, when his life has so deteriorated and his most precious things have been taken from him will he be shaken up to the point where he will seek out help. Only God knows just what that one specific thing is. Each person's "rock bottom" is different.

I once heard an alcoholic tell a story at an AA meeting that I would like to share. I hope I get it right...

One morning an alcoholic opened his eyes, only to be welcomed with a really bad hangover. Holding his head in his hands he groaned, "Oh, God. I have got to quit drinking. I'll do anything. What do you want me to do?"

Suddenly, to his amazement, a bright light appeared in his room. It was God.

"Do you really want to quit?" God asked.

"Yes! I'll do anything," the man begged sitting up in his bed.

11 Do's and Don'ts

"Anything?"

"Yes, I'll do anything."

"Okay. Do you have a truck?"

"Yes."

"Give my your truck, and you will become sober."

"I can't give you my truck. If I don't have my truck, I can't get to work."

"Oh, you have a job? Give me that, too."

"My truck and my job?! You've got to be kidding. If you took these I wouldn't be able to make the mortgage payments on my house! I'd lose the house!"

"So, you have a house? I want that, too."

"No, God. The price is too high. If I lost my job, my truck and my house, my family would be homeless."

"You didn't mention you had a family. Give me your family, too."

"Lord, I can't give you all these things."

"Then, you are not ready to get sober. Let me know when you are ready."

And with that, the light was gone...

Wow. This is so true. So many times an addict must lose everything before he is ready to humble himself to do whatever it takes to get well. Something will have to shake him to his core before he seek help. He will have to get to the point in his life to where he would be willing to give up everything in order to get the help he needs.

So, is there any way we can help speed up this process?

Yes there is, but it won't be easy. This is probably the hardest thing you will ever do. Be prepared to go through a lot of pain, fear, abandonment, and loads of discouragement. You will need all the support you can get from Al-anon, family, friends and hopefully a good counselor that understands the addictive relationship.

Here is a list of do's and don'ts for your alcoholic.

1. Do let him suffer the consequences of his mistakes.
2. Don't do his dirty work for him. Don't call in sick for him and lie about why he's not going to work.

Part 2: Helping the Alcoholic

3. Don't stay home from your work, just because he's having a bad hangover.
4. Don't bail him out of jail.
5. Don't pick him up from detox early, even though he'll have a ton of excuses why he needs to leave.
6. Don't pay his bills for him.
7. Don't try to patch up broken relationships between him and his kids, family, and friends.
8. Don't defend your husband or try to create situations where he is protected from the natural consequences of his behavior. This will be hard, because we are so afraid of his anger and rejection.
9. Do allow him to make his own decisions. This may be one of the hardest things you ever do. As codependents, we have this thing about solving problems. We need to remember he's not a two year old. You are not his mama. He's a grown man that can make his own decisions.

    My counselor kept telling me, "How old is he?"
    "52."
    "I think he's old enough to make his own decisions," she would say.
10. Do consider arranging to have a trained professional sponsor an intervention. Generally speaking, an intervention is when you have an expert interventionist work with your family and those close to the addict to confront the alcoholic about his drinking and its consequences with the intent of getting into a rehabilitative program. You schedule a meeting where the participants tell the addict that they love him, but will no longer allow his addiction to alter their lives. This is done in love and boundaries are set. Arrangements have previously been made for a detox center to be ready to accept him in case he accepts your help. This option can be costly, but apparently it has been somewhat successful for many. Many experts feel this option is not as successful as allowing the alcoholic to "hit the bottom" on his own, and has a high rate of drinkers returning to alcohol when they are released from the program.

11 Do's and Don'ts

11. Do allow time for the natural consequences of the disease to take place. Many therapists feel that allowing the alcoholic to experience the natural consequences of this sickness is the best type of intervention. This process allows the alcoholic time to truly hit his bottom, and according to most psychotherapists, this is the most successful intervention. The downside of this type of intervention is that it may take years to take place.
12. Do pray like crazy and have others join you in prayer for your loved one. God can lead your alcoholic to a place of submission. Remember, your drinker is not a weak-willed person. He may not be rational, but he can be stubborn and opinionated. Only God can break through this type of arrogance.
13. Don't yell at him or argue with him. This just gives him an excuse to drink more.
14. Don't allow yourself to get caught up with his crazy talking when he's drunk. If he starts pushing your buttons, which he will, leave for a while. Say you have to go to the bathroom or go buy some milk. More than likely he'll be passed out on the couch when you return; thus avoiding needless conflict.
15. Don't dump out his booze. He'll buy more, and it will just cost you more money in the end. It will also give him an excuse to drink, because you're so mean to him.
16. Don't follow him around the house with Alcoholic's Anonymous literature. He needs to want to get well on his own. It's not your job to tell him how to go about doing that.
17. Don't call him and ask him where he is and when he'll come home. Don't go searching for him.

Now, here is a list of things you can do or not do for you. If you do them, you will be healthier, which in turn will enable you to help your alcoholic.

1. Do deal with your fears of abandonment and rejection. You probably had issues with your father. You may have felt you were never good enough for him, abused by him, or for some

Part 2: Helping the Alcoholic

reason he was never available to you. Unfortunately, this has had an affect on your marriage relationship. As a result of your poor father-daughter relationship, you learned to accept unacceptable behavior. As a child you had no say in how you were treated. You had to cope in the best ways you knew how. Now as an adult, you will need to learn to value yourself enough to *not* accept abusive or hurtful behavior towards you and your children by your alcoholic husband. It is time to let go of your fears and move forward. Lay all your fears at the feet of Jesus. He will never reject or abandon you. He is your protector and provider. He will show you what to do.

2. Do learn to set boundaries. In the past, you may have allowed your husband to physically abuse you, threaten you with finding another woman or threaten to divorce you. He knew how to get you "back in line." That ends now. You must learn to protect yourself and your children. This is a huge scary undertaking, but you will be able to do this over time — with a lot of support and counsel.

3. Do rediscover who you are. For years my world revolved around my husband and his wishes, but for some strange reason everything was always my fault anyway. I was never good enough for him. This was his way of putting himself up on a pedestal and keeping me beat down. Over time, I have rediscovered my old before-marriage self. I have once again taken up sewing, guitar lessons, gardening, and keeping chickens. It is great. My focus changed from trying pointlessly to please an alcoholic husband to enjoying the gifts God has given me and blessing others with those gifts. You will discover a joyful, peaceful contentment as you set your happiness on things above, rather than on things below.

4. Don't obsess about your drinker and his problems. Live your own life. Leave him to his.

So, for those of us that feel we need to be fixing every little situation that comes along, I have given you a list of things you can work on.

This is not an easy list. It will take the power of God to accomplish. Hang in there. You are growing stronger everyday.

11 Do's and Don'ts

Are you the type that feels she must control every situation? If so, why do you think you are like this?

Describe your relationship with your father.

Part 2: Helping the Alcoholic

Which items from the list of do's and don'ts for your alcoholic do you need to work on?

Which items from the list of do's and don'ts for you do you need to work on?

Write a prayer for power to accomplish your new goals.

12 LOVING FROM THE TOP DOWN

"Praise be to God, who has not rejected my prayer or withheld his love from me!"
Psalm 66:20

One morning during my devotions, I was lamenting the fact that I was beginning to feel happy inside. Dare I say even a tad bit joyful? It scared me. I wasn't so sure I liked it.

Here I am living separated from my alcoholic husband, and before, when I was alone like this, I would be so lonely. I'd have a physical pain deep in my heart all the daylong. I hated being separated from him. Yes, I will confess I was somewhat clingy.

I decided to talk to God about this, because I felt guilty for feeling joyful. I felt like I was losing my love for my husband. I didn't want to do that. I wanted to stay married. I wanted him to discover sober living, for me to recover from my co-dependency, and for us to reunite someday. If I really loved him, why was I beginning to feel happy while we were still separated? It didn't make sense.

Well, I discovered that what I was experiencing was a form of detachment, and there was nothing wrong with feeling that way. In fact, it was all right. I was learning to love from the top down, instead of from the bottom up. Huh? What'd you say? What am I talking about? Well, here's how God explained it to me.

"Love is like a box of chocolates. You never know…" No, just kidding. Excuse me, Forrest…

Love is like a jar sitting on the front porch in the hot sun on a lazy summer afternoon. Your husband is inside the jar. You can love him from the bottom up by being clingy like sticky honey down in the bottom of that

Part 2: Helping the Alcoholic

jar. When you do this, you can never fully love him. He moves around trying to get away from you. You can love his foot one day, and his leg the next, and if you get really romantic, maybe up to his neck, but never all of him at once. Truly, he is in control of how much love will flow between the two of you, and you are at his mercy. He can stamp around in the jar, scrape the honey off of him, or trample all over you. Your life feels out of control.

But, here's the good part, you can love him from the top down instead. You can be the lid and jar its self. As a lid, you are getting your love mainly from the Son. If you know the son of righteousness, God, our Father, He will beam down his warmth all over that lid and jar. The jar is like your heart. He warms your heart so much; you radiate your warmth and love all over those you come in contact with inside your space (the jar).

Yes, some love will come up to you from your husband, but what you get from him will pretty much just be a reflection of you, because he will be incapable of generating that heat himself, because he has no connection with the Father. You can radiate the warm of your love all over him no matter how much he dances around in that jar, whether he likes it or not. If you don't receive it in return, it's okay. You are still soaking in God's love, and you are so saturated with it, you don't need your husband's love to be fulfilling your need of love. It's all good.

In fact, it's wonderful to bask in God's love, because you will come to love your drinker purely for the joy of sharing God's love with him. His reaction to it will make not a bit of difference to you, because the love is coming from above. Not from him. Not from you, but from God. There will be no manipulating or mothering in your interactions with him. There will be no begging for his love, nor crying out for his attentions. You will just be a little bundle of joy. People will love being around you.

This new you will amaze him. He won't know what to think about your new attitude. At first, he will doubt your genuineness, but eventually, he will see that his actions no long affect how you react. He will feel like he has lost control of you and will wonder if you are seeing another man. You are. Jesus. He will be unlike your drinker. God will fulfill your every need and love you undconditionally.

I'm sure you've heard the word "detachment" before. I used to wonder what exactly that meant. Now, I understand. It is total surrender to the love

12 Loving From the Top Down

of God — a wild abandonment of self and circumstances. It's basking in God's love and trusting in Him fully. It will be good for your marriage.

Hmmm. So, I'm a jar, huh? Well, as long as the Son is shining on me, I'm good, and all those in whom I come in contact will be thankful that I am a jar.

What does "loving from the top down" mean to you?

Write a plan to love your alcoholic from the top down.

PART 3: HELPING YOURSELF

13 HAVE NO OTHER GODS

You shall have no other gods before me. Exodus 20:3

Just as we fear God, we fear our alcoholics. This is not right.

Have you or your kids ever said the following?

"I just got off the phone with my husband, and I'm shaking like a leaf."

"The pain in my stomach begins every time I get within a mile from my home."

"I never know what I am coming home to."

"Mom, is Dad in a good mood?"

Sound familiar? Alcoholics make a valiant effort to keep their families whipped into shape. As a result, we are often afraid of making mistakes, which might trigger a rage. We diligently work to meet their expectations, solve their problems and keep them happy. The entire family tiptoes through life on eggshells in fear of the next big explosion.

Alcoholics seem to instinctively know what will hurt our feelings the most – how to push our buttons. This is the ammunition they use to keep us feeling inferior, and they will hone in on it like a vulture onto road-kill.

Personally, I am sensitive to my husband's flirting with other women — especially right in front of me. So, of course, that's what he specializes in. I've told him countless times it hurts my feelings, so instead of stopping he increases this irrational behavior. I am also sensitive about my weight, so he searches for ways to make sarcastic remarks about my need to lose weight.

Why does he hurt me time and time again? What kind of payoff does he get from hurting the one he supposedly loves more than anyone else in the world?

13 Have No Other Gods

It's because he loathes himself and what he has become. His self-esteem is very low. He figures if he can bash you and the kids down enough, he will look more in control and together than you.

You will find he does not do well around self-confident people. He understands they can see clearly through his lies. This scares him. He will try to think of an excuse to leave the presence of people with this kind of confidence.

Sometimes physical and/or emotional abuse is involved as a part of his control. This may be a fearful and dangerous time. This is when it is time to step in and protect yourself and your children.

I remember the first time my alcoholic hit me. Our family was on a camping trip to the Grand Canyon. Our two children were probably about three and four. We had just finished doing our laundry in town and everyone was tired and cranky. As we began our trip back to the campsite, it wasn't long before the girls began arguing in the back seat. This was the last straw for my husband, and he began yelling at them to shut up. Suddenly, he turned around and started pounding them all over, while he was driving. I yelled at him to stop, and he slapped me in the face — hard. I was shocked. The kids were squalling, but at least he stopped. I had always told myself that if my husband ever hit me, it would be the first and last time. Well, here we were in the middle of a national forest, and I had no money and nowhere to go. I slept in the girls' tent that night. Things were very strained and quiet for the rest of vacation and our trip home. The girls quickly forgave, as children often do, as did I, and life went on.

At some point in this relationship, I am going to have to take my soul back. I am going to have to realize that my emotional and physical health is essential to the well being of my children and family. I am accountable to God for my children and myself.

Regaining control of my life is going to take some real one-on-one time with God and the support of those who love me.

I will pray for Him to reveal to me areas in which my alcoholic has taken over my life. Then, take it back. My spouse is not my god.

I will seek out help from friends, counselors, and family. I may need to stay with them for a while until the smoke clears and I can regain some sanity.

Part 3: Helping Yourself

I read this same advice when I was searching for help in my relationship, and I thought, Yeah, right. Just exactly how am I supposed to do that without getting killed? I can write this laughingly now, but seriously, at the time, getting killed really was a possibility.

Here is a thought that finally worked for me. As soon as I saw that my alcoholic was in a stinking mood, I would leave. Go outside for a walk, clean the bathroom, go get the mail, go visit my parents or a friend… Just get physically away from him for a time.

We're addicted to our addict. He has become our drug of choice, but it's now time to wake up and see things as they really are. Tear down that pitiful tin god. I know, "Easier said than done." But we can do it, through the support of others and by the grace of God!

What are some of your sensitive buttons your alcoholic likes to push?

Why do you think he pushes these buttons?

13 Have No Other Gods

Write some ways you can respond differently, when your alcoholic pushes your buttons.

If your alcoholic has become your addiction, what are some ways to let go of this addiction safely?

Where can you go for help when things get out of control?

Part 3: Helping Yourself

14 BOUNDARIES

If any of you lacks wisdom, he should ask God, who gives generously to all without finding fault, and it will be given to him. James 1:5

I had heard about boundaries early on in my marriage in some of the marriage books that I read. They sounded like something I'd like to do, but never could figure out how.

Boundaries are "lines drawn in the sand, " so to speak, which have consequences if crossed. They can be verbalized, or they can be understood without saying a word. You remember — like the bully at school...

"Hand over your lunch money!"

You knew the consequences without his having to go into great detail about how many ways he was going to pound into a fine powder, if you didn't hurry up and hand over the money. At other times, boundary consequences were clearly outlined for us. You remember — like the alcoholic you know...

"If you don't get your #$@% out here, I'll come in their and kick your @#$!"

Interestingly, alcoholics seem to have no problems setting boundaries for their families. They bellow loudly, wield big sticks, and are adept at intimidating us by using colorful language, threats, and wild, flailing gestures. Sometimes, they even use force in a variety of physical ways.

My husband once told me the reason he yelled at me so much was because that's when I listened the best. Wow. Obviously, I had set no boundaries there. Yelling worked for him, and I didn't object. I actually rewarded his efforts by staying there and listening even harder. My pathetic reaction reinforced his yelling to be an effective way to get my undivided

14 Boundaries

attention. My standing there, while under attack, was a choice I made. Looking back, I should have respected myself enough to stand up for myself, and walked away. I finally, came to understand that my remaining in the room and taking the abuse was a sin. I was allowing God's princess to be violated by not leaving; therefore, grieving my Father, by not protecting his precious loved one, me.

It seems that people in relationships with alcoholics often have difficulties setting limits on what is acceptable behavior toward them, and what is not. We are the meek, mild, beaten-down co-dependent spouses who shake violently in our boots while being battered – even afraid to look our assailant in the eye. This is often the result of years of intimidation, threats, and physical and emotional abuse. Often, we are in no condition to take a stand for our children or ourselves, because if we do, there will be physical or emotional negative consequences.

> *"Do you not know that your bodies are temples of the Holy Spirit, who is in you, whom you have received from God? You are not your own; you were bought at a price. Therefore honor God with your bodies." 1 Corinthians 6:19, 20*

Setting boundaries sounded like a good coping strategy to me, but I had no idea how to carry out the consequences. What type of consequences should I set down for which behaviors? I didn't have a clue, and because I was terrified of abandonment, violence, and rejection, I laid low and took the abuse for many years — with very little to no objection.

Eventually, I learned that in order to be strong enough to set boundaries, I was going to have to overcome years of deep-seated fears. I knew I couldn't do it on my own; so, I sought help and surrounded myself with emotional support. I joined Al-Anon, found a sponsor and began the twelve-step process of recovery for myself. In so doing, it soon became apparent that fear was one of my greatest enemies.

My sponsor suggested that I didn't really know God, because I had fears. Woah! That scared me. Seriously? I thought I had a great relationship with God. What did she mean by that?

She went on to explain that the Bible says, *"God is love..."* and *"perfect love casteth out fear."*

Part 3: Helping Yourself

I began to prayer three times a day for my fear to be removed from me. I claimed the promises found in Joshua 1 where God repeatedly commanded Joshua to be strong and courageous. I wanted that kind of strength.

I am a princess of the Almighty King and have a right to be treated with dignity. No one has the right to harm my children or me. This is not selfishness! This is honoring my Father. I have the right and obligation to protect them and myself.

After about one week, I began to feel a change in my emotions. I began to experience a newly found peace and confidence I had never felt before. The feeling came gradually over the course of the next few weeks as my faith in God grew. I began to really know that God was going to be with me no matter what. I had nothing to fear, but fear its self. Yes, I was becoming courageous!

***Be strong and courageous**, because you will lead these people to inherit the land I swore to their forefathers to give them. **Be strong and very courageous**. Be careful to obey all the law my servant Moses gave you; do not turn from it to the right or to the left, that you may be successful wherever you go. Do not let this Book of the Law depart from your mouth; meditate on it day and night, so that you may be careful to do everything written in it. Then you will be prosperous and successful. Have I not commanded you? **Be strong and courageous. Do not be terrified; do not be discouraged**, for the Lord your God will be with you wherever you go. Joshua 1:6-9 [boldface added for emphasis]*

"Grrrrrr." I had received strength like a lion. And so through the empowerment of the Holy Spirit, I decided to set down my first consequence.

My first consequence may seem silly to you, but it wasn't for me. First a little background…

One bright sunny day, when my husband and I were on our honeymoon, we decided to go hiking in the Yosemite National Forest. After about five minutes, I was astonished and dismayed when my newly acquired protector and provider took off around the bend in the trail. He bounded along at a breakneck speed leaving me in the dust without a

14 Boundaries

backward glance. I was left behind to be eaten by wolves, or to be raped by a gang and my limp dead body flung over a cliff. Perhaps I would be kidnapped by an ax murder and my body parts fed to the vultures. As you can see, my fears were running wild, and I was devastated and discouraged that my new husband cared so little for my well being.

I slowly made my way up the trail alone with tears stinging my eyes. I remember not looking up when people passed me on the trail for fear they would see my swollen, wet eyes or red, puffy face.

Meanwhile, my intrepid husband had made it to the end of the trail. I was not a happy camper when I finally caught up with him at the end of the trail. There stood my valiant husband — casually leaning against a tree chatting it up with some lovely young ladies. He didn't even bother to glance my way. Well, you can imagine how the rest of our honeymoon went. So, was the beginning of a not so beautiful relationship…

So, you can see why taking walks together have been a bone of contention in our marriage ever since that incident.

In later years, when I had the courage to tell my husband how I felt about his behavior on this trip and similar behavior on other hiking trips, he told me the way he saw it was that since he was the boss, I should have kept up with him or stayed in the car. There was no discussion, and I being the co-dependent little wife that I was thought maybe he was right. Maybe, I should have been more submissive, more respectful, and a more loving wife. How wrong I was…

Now that I had my dignity and courage back, I made up my mind that I didn't want to go through those feelings any more. I was no longer going on walks with him if that meant being left behind or having him snap branches in my face. If he wanted to take walks like that, more power to him, but not with me. I was able to set this new boundary kindly and in a loving way, using "I statements."

I told him that it hurt my feelings when he walked ahead of me, and I didn't like it when he smacked branches in my face. If he wanted to walk like that, go ahead. No, I didn't want to go for a walk with him. You'd never guess what happened next.

He said, "Okay. I'll walk with you," and he did. We walked together for the first time in 25 years. It was great. Unfortunately, he started backtracking and going ahead, and smacking branches again; so, I said, "No I don't want to go anymore. I don't enjoy it," and that was that. I go alone or with my daughters or friends now.

When you set boundaries, don't shriek out obscenities and tell them they're bums for treating you like they do. They are grown up and have a right to act however they want. You have the right to accept how they act or leave it. Your reaction and your boundaries are your own business. You are in charge of you, and you can only change you; so, that is where you need to begin.

The whole process is simple really. The consequences don't have to be crazy, insane, difficult, or confrontational. Just kindly tell him how you feel, and that you are no longer going to put yourself in that position, because you don't like it. Then don't. That's all there is to it. It's not rocket science.

You are of great value, and should be treated as the child of God that you are. The same goes for your children. Sometimes, they are unable to protect themselves; so, it's your responsibility to protect their dignity, too.

Once, when our two daughters were about four and five years old, they got up in front of the church to sing a song. It was just the two of them dressed in their best church dresses with me directing. Before any words came out, they became nervous and starting giggling, looking at each other, and trying to hide behind each other. They did eventually start singing, and it was as if sweet melodies from heaven had burst into that old grey-headed church. Wrinkled faces were beaming and nodding with pleasure. As the song came to an end, I was proud that the girls had gone through with it, and our daughters were ecstatic to be done with it. As we made our way back to the pew amid enthusiastic, "Amen's." I noticed my husband lips were pressed tightly together. He refused to even look at us. He spat out the words under his breath, "What was wrong with them. I can't believe they acted like that!"

When we got into the car after the services were over, he let them and I know in no uncertain terms just how ashamed he was of us, and we had better straighten up next time and show him proud. Needless to say, I was furious at him. I set down some consequences right then and there. My daughters would never have to put up with that kind of behavior from him again; so they never sang for church again.

14 Boundaries

Looking back on that experience, I realize now that that was not the right consequence, but it was the best I could do at the time. It was my way of protecting my children.

I should have realized that my children were being emotionally and physically abused back then and set boundaries with rational consequences or left. I wish I knew then what I know now, but I didn't. I don't beat myself up about it. I know I did the best I knew how.

I have since asked forgiveness from my grown children and from God for staying in that situation. I have received their pardon.

One more thing about boundaries... Be easy on yourself. Don't expect yourself to be strong all at once, or to automatically know what consequences there needs to be for unacceptable behavior. Pray about it. Seek counsel from godly friends and family, search the scriptures, and sound Christian literature for help. Surround yourself with support and lovingly move forward with courage. God has promised to give you wisdom.

What are boundaries?

Name some things your drinker does that offend you.

Part 3: Helping Yourself

Choose the one action he does that offends you the most in your list above. Write what you can do to set a boundary to protect yourself.

What consequences to your boundary to you expect to happen?

What will be your reaction? Remember. Do not be confrontational… You can carry out your consequence quietly and with dignity.

15 OBSESSIVE THINKING

For this is what the Sovereign Lord says: I myself will search for my sheep and look after them. As a shepherd looks after his scattered flock when he is with them, so will I look after my sheep. I will rescue them from all the places where they were scattered on a day of clouds and darkness... I will search for the lost and bring back the strays. I will bind up the injured and strengthen the weak... Ezekiel 34: 11, 12, 16

Have you ever "obsessed" over your alcoholic? I mean, have you ever had thoughts such as, "I wonder where he is. Is he drinking? Is he thinking about me? Is he hurting as much as I am? Does he miss me? What is he doing? Who is he with?" If so, you are not alone; I have had these very same thoughts.

During one of our many separations, I remember turning these thoughts over and over again in my head. They were continuously with me day and night.

My energy and thoughts were being completely controlled by my constant obsession over this man. I felt like I couldn't function normally, and I was going crazy! I knew I had to find a way out, or else I was going to completely go insane.

Unfortunately, I found out that knowing that I needed to do to "get a life" and actually being able to do it were two very different things.

I had researched living with an alcoholic enough to know that obsessing wastes not only my time, but also keeps me from spending constructive, quality time with my friends, family and work. Yes, I knew it was bad for me, but I had no idea how to stop it, and even though I wanted to quit, I just didn't seem to have the right tools to give up my obsessive behavior.

One day, my Al-Anon sponsor and I decided to try and figure out why I was having so much difficulty "letting go and letting God." After an in-depth self-study within Al-Anon's fourth step, we came up with an answer.

For me it all came down to three main things — fears, my lack of self-esteem, and a lack of faith in God.

First of all, let's discuss about my fears. I discovered I feared rejection and abandonment. I was afraid my husband might leave me for another woman. That he wouldn't love me anymore, would find another, move out, and leave me all alone. Hmmm. I think we were onto something.

Digging a little deeper, we found out that underlying this fear were feelings that I was not good enough to deserve a good relationship.

I imagine my low-self esteem began during my childhood and strengthened during my 25-year marriage to an alcoholic. As a child, I was never good enough to win my father's approval. I missed this and sought after it, until I was a teenager. Then, my attitude kicked in, and I became "Miss Tough Girl." Who needed his approval anyway? Me. That is who. I was just too naive to recognize it wasn't my problem. It was my father's.

I find it pretty amazing that almost all the women in alcoholic relationships I have talked to, do not have a healthy relationship with their fathers. In fact, they are like me. Either he was totally non-existent in their lives, or else they wished he were.

After I married my husband, he carried on the tradition of treating me like I was his possession to be used and abused as he saw fit. For years, I was told all our marriage problems were vastly my fault, and, of course with my being as mentally sick as I was, I believed him. In retrospect, that's probably why I married him. He treated me in a way that was familiar to me.

Facing these fears for what they were – lies from Satan, made me realize these fears had to go. They were not from the Lord, but from the great deceiver, Lucifer. I wanted to let go of them, but didn't know how, and if I did, then maybe my fears would come true. Then what?!

My sponsor suggested that, if I loved hanging on to my fear so much, why didn't I just pray for God to give me more fear. Well, okay. Wait a minute. That's not right! Or was it?

The more I thought about it, the more it made me sick to my stomach. I felt like throwing up!

15 Obsessive Thinking

Suddenly, I remembered the text I had read before in the Bible about fear.

There is no fear in love. But perfect love drives out fear, because fear has to do with punishment. The one who fears is not made perfect in love. 1 John 4:18

Okay, if God is love, and He drives out fear, then that must mean he doesn't give us fear. So, praying for fear would be like praying for Satan to take over my life. Hold it right there. I couldn't do that! No, way!

These thoughts put my clinging to my fears into clear perspective. My fears were coming from Satan — not God. Satan was on a mission to discourage and destroy me. He wanted to keep me anxious and useless for the Lord's service.

Now, I wanted all fear in my life removed. I no longer wanted to entertain Satan – allowing him to cripple me with this insidious trait.

So instead of praying to keep my fear, I began praying for the fear to go. Many times a day — every time I began worrying about my drinker, I would pray for the fear to leave me and to be replaced with courage instead. That was a big switch — from fear to courage. After I began to see my fears morphing into courage, I began to see myself differently, too.

I once overheard my alcoholic husband telling one of our daughters, that he didn't respect or appreciate me like he knew he should. Ever since, these words have been swirling around in my head. Why didn't he?

Upon my reflection, I have come to the conclusion that his disrespect is primarily my fault. I have allowed him to verbally and physically abuse me for many years; yet, I still clung to him like a mud sucker on a shark. I was disgustingly dependent on a very sick person. I was making him my clay god, by irrationally searching for approval from someone incapable of giving it. I needed a reality check. Who was this person I was worshipping?

I thought to myself, "If he were someone that I was considering dating, would I?"

I gave myself a resounding, "You've got to be kidding! He wouldn't get a second glance from me!" He is an alcoholic-drug addict, who can't financially support himself; much less a family, who has hit me, yelled at me, cursed me in very colorful language, and has had numerous one-night affairs with various women. Yet, here I was — still claiming him as my one and only. Am I crazy?

Yes, I am. I have succumbed to the natural consequences of remaining in a relationship with an alcoholic. As they say in Al-Anon, "The definition of insanity is doing the same thing over and over and expecting different results."

My self-respect was gone down. I had believed the drinker's lies and clung to a fantasy world of what my marriage could be. I was stuck under a dark miserable damp rock; I couldn't see the light for which way to get out.

That's when God sent me supporters to help me out. They reminded me of my value, of my accomplishments, of what my dreams used to be, and where I could still go with my life. I hadn't thought of these things for decades.

Thinking of me was hard at first. Wasn't that being selfish — thinking of my needs? Oh, no! For God sees each one of us as His pearl of great price. I am the apple of His eye — His bright and shining star. I am someone of worth, and it is my responsibility to take care of God's awesome creation — me! Actually coming to believe this in my heart has been a gradual process, and I have had to be gentle with myself as I began the healing process.

The Lord your God is with you, he is mighty to save. He will take great delight in you, he will quiet you with his love, he will rejoice over you with singing. Zephaniah 3:17

Over time, as I learned to replace my fears with courage and my low self-esteem with pride in my lineage traced back to my Father in Heaven. I determined to trust Him who loves and understands my husband better than me. He has promised to search for him with a passion. It was high time I left my drinker to the Expert.

It was time for me to quit trying to control my drinker through my worrying, start valuing myself as God sees me, and trusting Him to do what is best for my husband.

Today, I have better things to think about — like being used of God to bless others. God's got this…

15 Obsessive Thinking

List some fears you have about your relationship.

Why do you think you have those fears?

Write the names of some people that love you and would be willing to support you in your recovery of your self-esteem. (You many wish to expand your list to include professionals, such as pastors or counselors.)

Part 3: Helping Yourself

Why are you valuable to your drinker?

Why are you valuable to your friends and family?

Why are you valuable to God?

Considering all of these answers, whom do you trust to keep your best interest in mind? Why?

16 FACING LONELINESS

You will keep in perfect peace those whose minds are steadfast, because they trust in you. Trust in the Lord forever, for the Lord, the Lord himself, is the Rock eternal.
Isaiah 26:3,4

If you are in a relationship with an alcoholic spouse, you understand what it is like to come face-to-face with loneliness. You feel emptiness in your heart and a pain in your chest that no one else can fathom. Sometimes, this hole in your soul feels worse than if you were divorced, or if he were dead, because it lingers. There is no end to it — no closure. It just goes on and on and on…

Loneliness is compounded by the fact that your alcoholic is always in your heart, but he is not always at home, nor in your life. He is totally distracted with his distorted reality. It's all about him.

You have no control over his actions. Even though he is an adult, he continues to make immature choices, which adversely affect his family.

The disease clouds his mind; he feels that all is well. You are just overly sensitive…

Even though you may love him with all your heart, the truth is, his sickness will not allow him to express love unless it is for a selfish gain. He is unable to understand that you feel abandoned and left behind — traded in for the bottle. Booze is his foremost romantic interest, his medicine for taking away his feelings of guilt and shame. There is no getting around it. It has a grip on him stronger that you can understand. Drinking comes before his family, God, and even himself.

So, where does that leave you? It feels like you are totally alone. Alone to take care of life's problems, alone to raise the kids, alone to take care of the finances, and alone to keep the home fires burning. If you have children, you are raising them as a single parent in almost all respects. There is injustice in that, and it makes you angry. How can you get over these feelings?

If you are really blessed, you may have loving family members or friends living nearby or that you can call or visit. This can help. Good relationships may decrease loneliness for periods of time, but they don't take it away permanently.

How else can you combat loneliness? Well, you could divorce, or have an affair, but these would ultimately intensify the pain and cause even more problems. Loneliness wouldn't disappear. It would become more complicated, and shame and guilt would be added to your feelings of isolation. As Christians we know these are not the answers.

I have found there is only one way to feel comfort and peace. The was is to trust God and turn our lives completely over to our Lord and Savior. He's not called our "Savior" for nothing, you know…

Trust that all is in God's hands. Hold onto Him for all your worth. Cling to His precious promises. Rest in the assurance that he loves you, is crazy in love with you, and will bless you.

"For I know the plans I have for you," declares the Lord, "plans to prosper you and not to harm you, plans to give you hope and a future. Then you will call upon me and come and pray to me, and I will listen to you. You will seek me and find me when you seek me with all your heart. I will be found by you," declares the Lord, "and will bring you back from captivity…" Jeremiah 29:11-14

Take your eyes off your alcoholic for a minute. Look around you at the blessings God has showered upon you. Look at your children, your family, your job, how he has supplied your needs. Have you remembered to spend time with your Creator? Have you thanked him for getting through those long, lonely nights? For putting food on your table and gas in your car when there was no money? Praise Him. Sing Him a song.

Praise be to the Lord, for he has heard my cry for mercy. The Lord is my strength and my shield; my heart trusts in him, and I am helped. My heart leaps for joy and I will give thanks to him in song. Psalm 28:6-7

16 Facing Loneliness

Rest assured He is working this very minute in your behalf. It may not be in the ways you think he should, but God knows better than us. You are where you are supposed to be right now. He knows exactly where your alcoholic is right now. He is standing there with him, because of your prayers and the prayers of the saints over them. He knows what is going on. He knows you long for peace and serenity and love. He is there for you. Take his hand. Hop up into his lap and lean firmly into his strong embrace. He loves you and will bear you up. You will live, laugh, and love again.

But those who hope in the Lord will renew their strength. They will soar on wings like eagles; they will run and not grow weary, they will walk and not be faint. Isaiah 40:31

We need to put it all in His hands and rest in His love. Think — today, I am lonely and sad, but I choose to trust that God is in control of my life and has a beautiful plan already laid out for my future. I will choose to praise Him for what is to come and the blessings that have been. I will look for His love that is displayed today.

Go to Him in prayer, and tell Him all about your loneliness. Remember, He is your best friend — a husband for the widows, which you essentially are. You have lost your real husband to the bottle.

For your Maker is your husband— the Lord Almighty is his name— the Holy One of Israel is your Redeemer; he is called the God of all the earth. Isaiah 54:5

Go to God in prayer or spend some quiet time with Him in nature. Listen to Him whisper sweet nothings into your ears in the wind. Listen to him sing his love songs to you in the light trill of the songbird. Feel his arms of love around you in the warmth of the sun. Lie in the fresh green grass and feel his arms wrapped tightly around you. And rest... Aaaaaah. Only then can you find true serenity.

The Lord is my shepherd, I lack nothing. He makes me lie down in green pastures, he leads me beside quiet waters, he refreshes my soul. Psalm 23:1, 2

Part 3: Helping Yourself

During what times have you felt the most alone in your marriage?

Write down names of family members or friends you can call or visit at your lowest times.

Write down some places where you can secretly meet with God in a natural setting to spend time with him.

16 Facing Loneliness

What day and time can you meet God regularly for spending time with Him?

Write a Bible verse of encouragement to remember during your loneliest times.

Part 3: Helping Yourself

17 SELF-RIGHTEOUSNESS

For I know my transgressions, and my sin is always before me. Against you, you only, have I sinned and done what is evil in your sight; so you are right in your verdict and justified when you judge... Hide your face from my sins and blot out all my iniquity. Create in me a pure heart, O God, and renew a steadfast spirit within me. Do not cast me from your presence or take your Holy Spirit from me. Restore to me the joy of your salvation and grant me a willing spirit, to sustain me. Psalm 51:3-4, 9-12

My counselor "slapped me upside my head" (figuratively) at my last session.

There I sat, pitifully bemoaning the fact that I didn't think my alcoholic husband was really completing AA's 12 steps as he claimed or the way I thought he should be. On top of that, he was being his usual selfish, thoughtless, irresponsible, pathetic self. Unbelievable! I was shocked!

My counselor just sighed, readjusted herself in her chair, looked pointedly at me and said, "I'm more worried about your recovery than his. You are clearly not ready to reconcile. You have a lot of 'house cleaning' to do before that can happen."

What?! (This is where the "slap" came in.)

I sat there staring blankly back at her, my mouth hanging open. "What do you mean?"

I honestly didn't know. I couldn't possibly imagine what I was doing wrong. My husband's sins were so blazingly apparent; my sins were not. I was the holy one — doing every thing a good Christian woman should do to hold her family together. Maybe, she'd missed the part about my husband...

17 Self-Righteousness

Thus began an hour-long session on seeing myself as I really was. I call this revelation my "light bulb experience."

And it was during this session that I discovered numerous "amends" I needed to make to my children, husband, family, and friends. I shamefully admit — I allowed my children to be raised in an abusive home.

Even though I did stand up to my husband when there was verbal abuse, and I would get in between them whenever they was threatened or actual physical abuse, I never took them out of the situation on a permanent basis. I would leave for a time and then go back, before the real issues were resolved or, a lot of times, even before we discussed them.

My counselor gently reminded me that my job as a mother was, and still is, to protect my children, and I had let them down. Now, it was time to "own up" to my part in the abuse — I permitted them to be continually hurt.

Even though my children are now grown and gone, I still needed to admit to them that I was wrong for not protecting them from abuse by removing them from the situation. I needed to ask their forgiveness.

The next sin I had to work on was airing my families dirty laundry to family and friends! Yes, I was a professional victim. I got a "high" out of watching the astonished looks from my friends and family when I told the latest horrific detail of my husband's irrational behavior. I felt validated when they told me how incredible it was that we were still together. I felt like a martyr for staying in the marriage under such bad conditions.

Marriage problems do exist in every family, but these problems need to be dealt with only within the walls of the home, with God, and with professionals. I was wrong to confide in my parents, my brothers, my sister, my in-laws, my husband's family members, church members, friends and anyone else who would listen. Our shortcomings were not their business. They could not fix the problems. They were not trained to understand the insanity of alcoholism and its effects. Sharing mistakes with those outside of the immediate family only hurts the family. It never helps it. I needed to stop doing this immediately!

Another area of concern was that I confided in my daughters about my feelings toward my alcoholic. Children suffer greatly when we try to make them our marriage counselors. They do not need to know all the details of our marriage problems. Secretly, I wanted them to choose sides — to reaffirm my actions toward my husband and be disgusted with the his. Children are not mentally equipped to be counselors, and it unfair to try and get them to take sides. Now, I understand how my behavior has attributed to ruining my children's relationship with their father. I loosened the ties of our family.

I needed to ask forgiveness from my children and husband for my error in judgment about this. This task wasn't easy, but I did it.

My next project was to rebuild my husband's respect for me. I discovered my lack of setting boundaries in my marriage was a huge factor in our breakdown of communication. Because of my fears, I found myself lying to my husband about my feelings and letting unacceptable behavior slide. This led to feelings of resentment and anger on both our parts, and over time, caused my husband to lose all love and respect for me. I learned it is very important in effective communication to stand up for what is right for me. I needed to ask my husband to forgive me for being dishonest and hurting our marriage by not stating my true feelings by setting boundaries to build our marriage up.

Next, it was time to forgive myself for seeing myself and treating myself as worthless. All my faults that my alcoholic had drilled into my brain over the years would echo in my mind repeatedly, "Who would want you? You are overweight. You forget everything..."

Thankfully, I learned that when I look at my self as worthless, I am putting down God's *very good* creation.

Then God said, "Let us make mankind in our image, in our likeness, so that they may rule over the fish in the sea and the birds in the sky, over the livestock and all the wild animals, and over all the creatures that move along the ground." So God created mankind in his own image, in the image of God he created them; male and female he created them. God blessed them and said to them, "Be fruitful and increase in number; fill the earth and subdue it. Rule over the fish in the sea and the birds in the sky and over every living creature that moves on the ground." Then God said, "I give you every seed-bearing plant on the face of the whole earth and every tree that has fruit with seed in it. They will be yours for food. And to all the beasts of the earth and all the birds in the sky and all the creatures that move along the ground—everything that has the breath of life in it—I give every green plant for food." And it was so. God saw all that he had made, and

17 Self-Righteousness

it was very good. And there was evening, and there was morning—the sixth day.
Genesis 1:26-31

Is God a liar? No! He made me; therefore, I am very good. In fact, I am a princess of the King. You are, too! He said it. Act upon it.

The Lord appeared to us in the past, saying: "I have loved you with an everlasting love; I have drawn you with unfailing kindness." Jeremiah 31:3

Bathe in His love. We are His.

Another area I needed to work on was being judgmental of my alcoholic and his friends. It seems my life's purpose was to fix my husband's weaknesses. Often, I found myself listening carefully to our pastor as he preached. My husband-fixing radar antennas were on high alert—searching for tiny bits of information that might be beneficial to my "wicked" husband. I would sneak peeks at him as I stoically sat next him to see if he were listening. All the while I was praying fervently that the Holy Spirit would speak to his heart during the sermon to change him and make him a better man. I prayed for his sins. I listed them in my prayer journal.

When he'd come home drunk, I'd self-righteously sleep in the other room to avoid the stink, or if I were angry enough, I'd throw his clothes out on the porch and lock the door. I wouldn't let him come home, if he were drinking. He could stay at his disgusting drunk friend's house.

I ignored his alcoholic friends when they came over. I looked them up and down in disdain like they were trash, and I was some kind of saint.

I was blind to the fact that I too was a sinner. No different from my husband and his alcoholic buddies. Sin is disconnecting from God, whether it is from becoming drunk, or gossiping to all the family about someone else, it's all the same to God.

How self-righteous and judgmental I was! I had some apologizing to do to my husband and his friends.

These were a few issues I needed to change in my own life. I was truly humbled and ashamed. God have mercy on me a sinner.

Part 3: Helping Yourself

What are your responsibilities for your children and their well-being?

Are you meeting these responsibilities? Write down some ideas on how you may meet these needs in a safe way.

Write down some names of people that you can call and talk over the rough patches of your marriage with. Do not write down your children's names or family members' names. Make sure your supporter is someone you can trust to keep things private.

17 Self-Righteousness

Write down a time you were dishonest with your alcoholic in order to preserve the peace.

What is another way you could have handled the situation and been honest?

Part 3: Helping Yourself

List 10 wonderful things about you.

Write down how you should treat your drinker and his friends. What would Jesus do?

18 PUTTING ON THE FULL ARMOR OF GOD

Finally, be strong in the Lord and in his mighty power. Put on the full armor of God, so that you can take your stand against the devil's schemes. For our struggle is not against flesh and blood, but against the rulers, against the authorities, against the powers of this dark world and against the spiritual forces of evil in the heavenly realms. Therefore put on the full armor of God, so that when the day of evil comes, you may be able to stand your ground, and after you have done everything, to stand. Ephesians 6:11-13

Sometimes, I feel like I am being sucked into the vortex of my husband's insane world. Excuses and promises are made; then, never kept. I am blamed for his mistakes. Accusations and curses are randomly spit out. Reasoning things out logically as a couple has become totally impossible. Conversations that start out in subdued tones, quickly escalate, and spiral into out-of-control shouting matches or violence. He is master of the crazy dance.

The crazy dance is the desperate, frenzied dance of demons. It is what Satan and his demons use to keep our alcoholics thinking they are right, that everyone else is wrong, and that they will win it all in the end and have fun in the process. It is explosively dangerous and highly toxic.

Satan is out to take our loved-one's soul. He will stop at nothing to accomplish his hideous goal; therefore, we need to realize that we are not wrestling with the flesh and blood of the alcoholic. He has joined forces with the devil, and we are no match for them. Satan has been perfecting "alcoholic damnation" for thousands of years.

Part 3: Helping Yourself

I have felt the thick dark, foul atmosphere that enshrouds my husband when he is drinking. When I leave his presence and enter another room, it is as if I am walking into a new, fresh, clean, and bright atmosphere. I believe it is because evil angels are surrounding him. The demons encircle him and torture his soul. He is a wounded sick man; so, he strikes out at me, or anyone in his way to ease his agony — in the same way an injured animal would. He is desperately looking for relief. Finding someone to dance the crazy dance with is his only reprieve. This is not a dance of two humans. It is a battle between good and evil. God and Satan are at war. The soul of the alcoholic is their prize. Although we are pawns in this war, we, can choose which side we are on.

It is time to prepare for combat between good and evil. In order to do this successfully, you will need to wear the best armor and use weapons available; yes, I am speaking of the armor of God…

Before we do anything else, let's consider the different parts of the armor of God.

Stand firm then, with the belt of truth buckled around your waist, with the breastplate of righteousness in place, and with your feet fitted with the readiness that comes from the gospel of peace. In addition to all this, take up the shield of faith, with which you can extinguish all the flaming arrows of the evil one. Take the helmet of salvation and the sword of the Spirit, which is the word of God. Ephesians 6:14-17

You will need to wear every part of this outfit to be successful. If you use it in part, you will remain vulnerable, but if you wear the full armor you will conquer.

Then you will know the truth, and the truth will set you free. John 8:32

Let's begin with the belt of truth. The belt of truth is what holds the whole outfit together. Who needs droopy pants during a war? Right? Not me. The distorted incoherent arguments that the alcoholic uses to excuse his behavior are not the truth. He misrepresents the facts, sidetracks, manipulates, and openly lies to you. Don't fall for the bait. Keep your mind wrapped around what is true. If he curses at you and says you are the worst thing that ever happened to him, don't believe him. Look to the facts.

18 Putting on the Full Armor of God

The truth is that he has chosen the path he's taken. He has chosen when to pick up another drink. It has absolutely nothing to do with you. The frontal lobe of his brain is so damaged from toxins, he cannot even begin to reason logically.

Trust in the Lord and do good; dwell in the land and enjoy safe pasture. Take delight in the Lord, and he will give you the desires of your heart." Psalm 37:3, 4

The breastplate of righteousness covers and protects your heart. If you do what is right, it may be painful, but it saves your life. This may require you to make some tough decisions about your living conditions. Are you and your children safe and at peace where you are? When you make a decision to do what is right when it comes to protecting your family, expect an angry reaction from your alcoholic. He will not be pleased. He will feel that he is losing control over you. If you leave, who can he blame? Who will support him? This is to be expected. The evil angels will put up a fight. They want you brought down, too. When they see you joining hands with the heavenly hosts; they will scream with anger and push your alcoholic to do whatever it takes, to keep you dancing the crazy dance.

But the breastplate of righteousness will protect your heart. You will not die. You may leave the battle wounded and lonely; but you will recover and abundantly prosper.

Let your gentleness be evident to all. The Lord is near. Philippians 4:5

I really love the shoes of peace.

Pushing buttons is an alcoholic's specialty. He knows just what it takes to get you angry, but you need to realize that anger, retaliation, and resentments on your part will be like adding gasoline to the fire of addiction.

Your drinker knows deep down that he is causing problems within the family, and he is hypersensitive to accusations and confrontational talk. Just leave him be. Instead, look upon your alcoholic with pity and sympathy when he lashes out. Try something new and different. Respond kindly and without malice.

Part 3: Helping Yourself

This doesn't mean be a doormat. That is NOT what I am saying. If there is any type of abuse, get away from it. Fast. We do not have to contribute to it, or abuse our alcoholic in return. Quietly leave, with your self-respect in tact. Don't take his erratic behavior personally. He is in pain. Leave him alone.

Now faith is confidence in what we hope for and assurance about what we do not see. Hebrews 11:1

Now, pick up and use that shield of faith. This is another protective device for our hearts. Hold on to a faith that guarantees that God will work in our behalf, answer our prayers, and use every opportunity possible to bring our loved one to give his heart to Him. Everything is in God's hands.

If we truly believe God is in control, and if we daily give our hearts and wills over to him, He will talk through us, work through our hands to bless others, and will move us to do His goodwill. We must trust that everything that happens is part of His bigger picture for our happiness. That is a faith, which protects us from a world of hurt.

Therefore, with minds that are alert and fully sober, set your hope on the grace to be brought to you when Jesus Christ is revealed at his coming. 1 Peter 1:13

The helmet of salvation is a protection for our heads and our minds. God has given us protection from the power of sin and those who hurt us. If we acknowledge His salvation, He has promised to protect our minds from being hurt, feeling rejected, and from believing ridiculous insults and accusations drinkers fling at us.

Get to the point to where you can imagine a bulletproof Plexiglas barrier surrounding you. Then, when he comes at you with those crazy dance steps of accusations, let those ridiculous remarks bounce off the imaginary glass. Don't allow them to affect you. All those irrational words just slide right down that glass. Consider the source and don't take it seriously. You wouldn't take an insane person yelling at you from a street corner seriously. Nor should you take your alcoholic seriously. He is insane, and it's the bottle talking — not the person you once knew and loved. Let it go. Allow your mind to be at perfect peace.

The Spirit, or Holy Ghost, is your comforter. It is God's presence in your life. The Holy Spirit protects your dignity. If you have the Holy Spirit in you, your character will radiate the fruits of the spirit.

But the fruit of the Spirit is love, joy, peace, forbearance, kindness, goodness, faithfulness, gentleness and self-control. Against such things there is no law. Galatians 5:22, 23

Finally, don't make any hasty decisions. Take time to think before you respond to the craziness your spouse or loved-one may display. Consider, "What would Jesus do?" before you act. Display justice towards others and have a loving, peaceful heart. You will find that others respect you more -- including your addict. You will respect yourself more as well, because you will not feel remorseful for reacting in unkind, resentful, or self-centered ways.

How do you know, wife, whether you will save your husband? Or, how do you know, husband, whether you will save your wife? 1 Corinthians 7:16

When you make the decision to no longer be sucked into your alcoholic's chaotic life, you will discover a safe haven of peace – God's arms of love. You will exhibit self-control, instead of reacting disappointingly to his behavior. You will look upon him with love and pity — instead of hate and disgust.

You will give his crazy dance over to God, where it belongs. Let God take care of it; then, you will have peace, and the healing can begin for you and your alcoholic.

Describe the atmosphere you feel when you are around a drinking alcoholic.

Part 3: Helping Yourself

Why do you think the atmosphere feels this way?

What are some of your drinker's tactics to push your buttons to start the crazy dance?

Which fruits of the Spirit would you like to exhibit as you interact with the drinker?

18 Putting on the Full Armor of God

Putting on the whole armor of God is the only way to exhibit the fruits of the Spirit. Which parts of the armor do you especially need to ask God to help you put on and keep on?

Write a prayer below requesting the armor of God.

Part 3: Helping Yourself

19 THE CHILDREN

I will instruct you and teach you in the way you should go; I will counsel you and watch over you. Psalms 32:8

Children are gifts from God on loan to us. We have been appointed their caregivers and teachers. We are responsible for molding their characters, self-esteem, and sense of security. With this in mind, we need to be aware that every decision we make affects our children in one way or another.

If you are married to, or are in a relationship with an alcoholic, you have a unique set of problems to deal with. There are issues of trust, finances, discord, safety, and security. Keep in mind that you are not the only one affected by the way you handle these troubles. The decisions you make, in order to deal with these problems, will have far-reaching and eternal results on your children. Before you do anything, consider your choices prayerfully and carefully.

Children are smarter than you may think. You may imagine you are hiding the chaos of alcoholism from them, but you are not. They see daddy come staggering home late at nights. They smell the alcohol on him. They hear his slurred angry words. They hear your quiet sobs. They notice the hugs and kisses aren't there anymore between Mommy and Daddy. They see and hear. They wonder and cry silently in their beds. They know.

They see daddy sleeping in late. They hear you call in "sick" for him. Daddy doesn't go to work as much as he used to. There isn't much food on the table. Their clothes are getting holes. They stay home instead of going on vacation. They see and hear. They wonder and cry. They know.

19 The Children

They hide when daddy comes home. They get hit when they make noise. They are yelled at, belittled, and cursed at. You cover their bruises with long sleeved shirts in the summer. You keep them home from school to cover the abuse. They see and hear. They wonder and cry. They know.

Daddy acts funny sometimes. He touches them where it makes them feel uncomfortable. They witness things that small eyes should never see. They are confused. He threatens them. He accuses them. They are quiet. The see and hear and feel. They wonder and cry. Don't be fooled. They know.

The problem is, when you pretend the trouble is just between you and your spouse, you are only fooling yourself, and as a result, your children suffer.

In their minds they think that somehow, it is their fault. Daddy is angry, because they were being too loud when they play, because they forgot to put our bikes away, because they made daddy mad when they made a "D" in math, and then he got mad at mommy. They feel that they cause family conflict. They blame themselves.

Don't let them blame themselves. Be open and honest with them. Talk with your children about what they experience. Put the blame squarely where it lies — on the disease of alcoholism. Be frank with them. Depending on their age, you can tell them as little or as much as they need to know, but don't pretend like everything is okay when it is clearly not.

Small children need to know that daddy is sick, and it's not the child's fault. Pray for the alcoholic with them. Explain to them that you love them and their daddy, and that you are doing the best you can.

Older children can understand more. They can see how the marriage relationship is being affected. You can be more candid with them about the details of the disease. Let them know what your plans are to protect them. Your children's best interest should be your priority as the parent.

Go to a Christian counselor alone, and if your counselor advises it, eventually take your children. Make sure the counselor specializes in alcoholic family situations. They are specially trained for these types of situations, whereas a regular counselor is not as knowledgeable.

If there are no counselors in your area that specialize in alcoholism, or you cannot afford a counselor, there is always Al-Anon. These meetings are free. You will hear many stories very similar to yours. I found out that all our stories were alike in most ways and different in a few ways. If you have teenage children, you may be blessed to have a local chapter of Ala-Teen your child can attend, while you attend Al-Anon. Your children need healing — just the same as you need it.

Unfortunately, violence or incest may be occurring in your family. If you suspect it, more than likely you are right. Don't deny it or try to protect the offending spouse. Don't be afraid to ask your child or even your alcoholic about it. Let your children know that you are on their side and will protect them at all costs. Then, take whatever steps are necessary to keep them safe.

It is your responsibility to remove your children from this situation. Their safety should be your number one concern. Be ready and willing to make the necessary changes to protect them. Prepare for it and then do it. Be quick and decisive.

If you have to leave your home in order to protect you or your children, do not fear. God is with you. He commands you to be strong and courageous.

Have I not commanded you? Be strong and courageous. Do not be terrified; do not be discouraged, for the Lord your God will be with you wherever you go. Joshua 1: 9

That is His promise. Cling to it. Memorize it. Write it down on a sticky note and put it on your dash in your car. Read it going and coming from work. Keep that lifeline of communication between you and God always flowing between heaven and earth. He will be with you and your family. You are not alone.

If you feel it has come to the point where you have to leave to protect the children from harm, know that moving out of an abusive situation is easier said than done, if your alcoholic is abusive. Do NOT attempt to leave without professional help.

You will need a strong support system. Seek out supportive family members, Al-Anon members, church members, and friends — anyone you know that has your best interest at heart. Let them know of the violence or

19 The Children

incest and accept their help. Now is not the time to be proud. Be receptive if they offer help.

Some friends or family members may offer to let you stay at their home while you get back on your own two feet. If not, there are shelters where you can go. If you find yourself short on cash, there is government welfare help available. Gratefully accept help — even if it is for a short time.

You can call the nationwide help hotlines listed on page 81, Appendix C. There are domestic abuse hotline, addiction hotlines, and alcoholic hotlines – among others. The trained professionals on the other end of the line are equipped with resources to help you out of your situation safely.

"Where there is a will there is a way." You can do it, and rest assured God will be with you every step of that way.

You may not need to move. There is a chance you may be able to persuade your alcoholic to move out, or you could file for legal separation where you could keep the house. You could go to court and get a restraining order. Some states have programs where you can have your alcoholic be picked up by the police and restrained for psychiatric evaluation and treatment, if he is a threat to himself or you. Any of these scenarios may allow you to remain safely in your house while removing the alcoholic.

If he hits you, you suspect incest, or if he beats the children, it is your responsibility to call the police immediately and have him arrested. This is for your family's safety. Keep in mind it is also for his good.

Be prepared for when he will call you all teary-eyed and remorseful begging you to drop the charges. Don't fall for the bait. He is just like the kid that got caught with his hand in the cookie jar. He is sorry for the consequences of being caught, but would do it again as long as he can keep getting away with it. He needs to suffer the natural consequences of his actions. Robert G. Ingersoll once said, "In nature there are neither rewards nor punishments—there are consequences." Going to jail is a consequence. Let it happen.

Each child is a precious gift from God. Let us love and protect them whatever the cost; so, when Jesus comes again in the clouds of glory, we can say, "Here are our children. We protected them and loved them. They know you and love you, Father." And He will smile and wink at us as He rejoices over our babies with us.

What are some things that have happened in your home that your children should never have witnessed or experienced?

Is it safe to keep your child in the home of your alcoholic? Why or why not?

19 The Children

What can you do to better protect your children?

What steps will you take to protect your children?

Part 3: Helping Yourself

20 CHOICES

The eyes of the LORD *are on the righteous, and his ears are attentive to their cry; but the face of the* LORD *is against those who do evil, to blot out their name from the earth. The righteous cry out, and the* LORD *hears them; he delivers them from all their troubles. The* LORD *is close to the broken hearted and saves those who are crushed in spirit. The righteous person may have many troubles, but the* LORD *delivers him from them all...*
Psalms 34:15-19

    This chapter is written specifically for those married to an alcoholic. You are in need of special help, but before reading this chapter, let me remind you once again that I am not a psychologist or a counselor. What I am writing here are thoughts and ideas I have learned from my own experiences and research. Please do not make any decisions without consulting a trained professional. That said, let's consider some choices you will need to make, whether it is in the best interest for you, your spouse, and your children to stay together, separate, or divorce.
    Staying together is an option you should consider, as it was God's original plan for marriage. Here are some pros and cons for sticking it out.
    Pros: You won't be as lonely as you will be if you leave. You won't have the hassle of finding another place and financial burden of renting it. You won't have to move all your stuff. It will be cheaper. There's a remote chance he will become sober.
    Cons: You will still have to deal with his insane behavior, and possibly be going insane with him. You may still be in danger, if your alcoholic is a

violent person. Your children may still be in danger. You will still have to deal with the drama, lying, sleepless nights, and manipulation.

So, there you have it. You can add more pros and cons of your own. Staying is a choice, but even this choice needs to be made prayerfully.

Separating is another choice. There are varying degrees of separation. You can go to the bathroom to be separated. You can go shopping for a couple hours, go to the beach for the weekend, or your parents for Thanksgiving week. It might be a good idea to handle separation in smaller increments and work your way up. That way, you can see how you like the idea.

I separated from my husband probably 10 times or more for varying reasons. The last time was for about a year. It's okay to separate, change your mind and come back.

I left for a weekend once, and came back. He never even knew I was gone. What?! Yep. That's the way it is with an alcoholic. They are too tied up with themselves to care less what you do... Sigh. Sad, but true.

Okay, so the pros and cons of separation are:

Pros: You get peace and quiet. You will no longer have knots in your stomach on your way home from work. You are safer, if your alcoholic is violent. Your finances may actually be better, because your alcoholic isn't sponging off of your salary. You get more sleep. Your mind and body become healthier.

Cons: Unless you find a place that is furnished, you will have to move your things from your old house to your new, or buy all new furniture. You will feel a deep loneliness (although your alcoholic isn't missing you, because he's too inebriated). Your alcoholic may harass you trying to find out where you are. It may be hard on your kids missing their dad, if they are too young to understand. Your alcoholic may find someone to take your place.

Your alcoholic is probably going to become really angry when he gets wind that you are wanting out. He will feel that he is losing control of you and the situation. Some alcoholics are violent and others are passive. Only you know your alcoholic's behaviors behind closed doors. So, plan accordingly. Remember, you and your children's safety comes first.

If you do decide to move out, never tell your alcoholic where you are. He may come to you crying – asking for your address. He may start screaming at you that you don't trust him. He will tell you he is not a stalker, and you can trust him enough to tell him. Don't do it. Remember that alcohol affects the mind; he is liable to do anything.

Unfortunately, separation is no fun. You will suffer. You will feel lonely. You will sit by the phone nights wishing that he would call. You'll have a sick feeling in the pit of your stomach for days on end. You will wonder if he is missing you as much as you are missing him. Your resolve may eventually wear down, and you will call him to see how he's doing just to hear his voice. When you do, he will become angry with you and tell you to come back or else.... Don't respond in anger. Just tell him that you have moved out for your own sanity, or better yet, just say you have to go and hang up the phone. Arguing is useless, exhausting, and stressful when you are dealing with an insane mind. When you hang up the phone, you will be shaking. Stay strong in the Lord.

You will be afraid that he will find someone else, which he might. If he does it will be with someone as sick or sicker than himself (no big threat there). Their relationship will be way worse than the one you were in with him; therefore, feel sorry for him.

Besides, it's hard to lose an alcoholic. Even if you do get to a point in your life where you don't want him to come back, he'll be showing up on your doorstep again and again and again. It is as if he has these radar antennas poking out of his head picking up the latest wife signals. He can sense when you are truly becoming independent of him. It scares the bageebees out of him! His little antennas stick straight up and electrical charges start shooting sparks into the air and a warning siren starts going off in his head.

Warning! Warning! I am picking up strong signals that her support system is getting stronger, and she may leave me for someone else. Quick! I must make contact with her at all costs. I will turn up my charms to try to woo her back into my control!

Oh you will see him again all right; whether you want to or not. It happens all the time — alcoholics suddenly pop back into your life as if you've never been separated. It happened to me personally — more times than I can count. I've even heard of it happening years after a divorce. The alcoholic still feels like he can get you back, if he tries and really wants to.

Sometimes, he does try, and sometimes, if you do, you will be sucked back into the sick relationship. Never fear. As soon as you begin to see what's going on more clearly after falling for the "hook," you can get back up, dust yourself off and get on with life as it should be...

You will soon realize that you have a sense of relief, peace and eventually you will feel hope. As time passes, you will begin to find yourself smiling again, remembering that you have long lost passions. One day, to your amazement, you will hear yourself laugh. The sick feeling in your stomach will subside and you will find that there is life after your alcoholic.

I remember the first time I heard myself laugh after I had moved out. It had been such a long time since I had heard that sound, it sounded foreign. That's pretty sad, when I don't even recognize the sound of my laugh anymore. That told me, it had been too long.

"But what if I make a mistake? What if I move out, don't like it, and want to move back?"

Then move back in. I did this so many times! I just couldn't stand being alone. Finally, I figured out that my being there did not help the situation at all. It didn't take me long to remember why I had left in the first place. So I moved out again. This was okay. I lived and I learned.

If you make a mistake, you just figured out what doesn't work. My counselor told me on numerous occasions, "You are going to make mistakes and lots of them. That's part of your recovery journey. Just pick yourself up, dust yourself off, and keep going. Your falls will get fewer and further between, and you will grow stronger." I have found this bit of advice to be true.

Another reason to consider separation is when there is physical and/or mental violence.

Do you not know that your bodies are temples of the Holy Spirit, who is in you, whom you have received from God? You are not your own; you were bought at a price. Therefore honor God with your bodies. 1 Corinthians 6:19, 20

This verse reminds us that we are responsible to God for caring for our own bodies. We can not allow someone to abuse our babies or us. If abuse is occurring to you or your children, you have an obligation before God to protect you and your children. Move out. Separate or divorce.

That's pretty straightforward. We have to let go. Trust God and do what He says. I know it will be hard. But we have to stay strong.

Now, what about the choice of divorce? This is a hard decision to make. It may have to happen for a number of reasons: financial reasons, infidelity, or physical abuse. But even if it does, divorce doesn't have to be final. If you are a believer and pray for this individual, God may work a miracle and your alcoholic may be healed from the disease. Later on down the road, you may wish to move back in with him, or you may decide to move on.

Finally, we come to the decision of divorce. It is a sobering thought to be sure. It is not what God intended, but neither is abuse, adultery, and the mental anguish that is an everyday occurrence when you live with an alcoholic.

Divorce may have to happen for a number of reasons: financial reasons, infidelity, or physical abuse. But even if it does, divorce doesn't have to be final. If you are a believer and pray for this individual, God may work a miracle and your addict may be healed from the disease. Later on down the road, you may wish to remarry him, or you may decide to move on...

Here are some pros and cons to consider about before making the decision to divorce.

Pros: If you leave due to adultery or abandonment, you will be free to remarry. Your children can get a better role model for a father, if you remarry a godly man. (Don't remarry another drunk.) You will have a chance to regain your sanity. Your alcoholic has a better chance at recovery without your enabling — although, he many find someone else to enable him. You will be at peace. You have a chance at having a happy rest of your life.

Cons: You will miss him. You will lose a drunken husband. (Oh, wait. Maybe, this one should be in the "pro" list.)

20 Choices

Personally, I felt I was bound to my alcoholic husband forever, unless he committed adultery. I had read in the Bible where that is what Jesus himself said.

Jesus replied, "Moses permitted you to divorce your wives because your hearts were hard. But it was not this way from the beginning. ⁹ I tell you that anyone who divorces his wife, except for sexual immorality, and marries another woman commits adultery. The disciples said to him, "If this is the situation between a husband and wife, it is better not to marry." Matthew 19:8, 9

So, I went many years wishing he'd just go ahead and have an affair already! Was that wrong to feel that way? I think many of you know what I mean. How about be in a fatal car accident? I must admit that scenario had also crossed my mind. How could I think such things about someone I loved so much? I told you my sanity was leaving me...

Then, one day my pastor showed me another verse, I had never noticed before.

But if the unbeliever leaves, let it be so. The brother or the sister is not bound in such circumstances; God has called us to live in peace. 1 Corinthians 7:15

Really? That means all these years he's threatened to leave me, I could have smiled and said okay, and it would have been okay for me to remarry? Hmmm. This was news to me. My husband had checked out years ago. He had already abandoned me to alcohol a long time ago. I was free to go. Wow.

There are surely so many ways you can choose when deciding where to go from here with your alcoholic relationship. You have been through so much already. Ideas I have mentioned here should just be a springboard for your own list of pros and cons for each.

Also, my beliefs about the Biblical direction for separation and divorce are my personal beliefs. You will need to prayerfully consider your own beliefs. Ask God to reveal to you how you should see things.

I instruct you in the way of wisdom and lead you along straight paths. Proverbs 4:11

Part 3: Helping Yourself

Our creator is a God of peace, and you need peace in your life whether through separation or divorce. Seek Godly counsel, study the scriptures, talk with God and take one step at a time. He will direct your paths and make them straight.

Every person's journey is unique and your own. Don't let anyone decide for you. You are the one that will live with the consequences.

Don't be afraid to take that initial step to sanity that God calls you to make. You will know what and when that step needs to be made. The future will probably be very hazy and you will not be able to discern what is ahead for you and your family, but don't be afraid. As Al-Anon says, "Take it one day at a time." God will open up what you need to know about your future when you need to know it. Take baby steps.

Either way you choose, your life will not be easier at first. It will become harder before it becomes easier, but that is the way it always is when there is change. Remember, if things don't change, they will remain the same.

Now, is that what you want?

Do you want to stay in an alcoholic relationship? If so, why?

If you choose to stay in the relationship, list some ways to retain your safety.

20 Choices

List some ways to retain your sanity.

What are your thoughts on separation?

What are your thoughts on divorce?

Part 3: Helping Yourself

Name at least two Godly people who can give you wise counsel on where to go from here.

Write a plan of action.

21 FINDING PEACE

I rejoiced greatly in the Lord that at last you renewed your concern for me. Indeed, you were concerned, but you had no opportunity to show it. I am not saying this because I am in need, for I have learned to be content whatever the circumstances. I know what it is to be in need, and I know what it is to have plenty. I have learned the secret of being content in any and every situation, whether well fed or hungry, whether living in plenty or in want. I can do all this through him who gives me strength. Philippians 4:4-13

Have you ever been ready to give up? I know I have. I have tried everything in my power to get my alcoholic to quit, or at least for me to be able to deal with his illness effectively; yet here I am, still in the middle of the battle — growing weaker by the minute. I am ready to surrender and wave my little white flag high.

So, this is what it is like to hand my life completely over to God. I have pleaded, screamed, reasoned, enabled, and a whole host of other "bright ideas" to get my alcoholic to stop. Nothing worked. I have hit my rock bottom and am finally ready to let it go.

"God, he's all yours," I breathe.

He replies, "About time!"

I wanted so badly for things to end differently — for my husband to become my "prince charming" that comes riding in on his beautiful white steed to save the day. I imagined him coming home, apologizing for all he has put his family through. I envisioned him becoming the priest of the home, conducting morning and evening worships, and attending church with our children and myself. I saw him being responsible, reliable, and supporting the family financially through a regular job. I imagined him offering a strong arm to lean on and showing an interest in what is going on within the family. I imagined him fixing things around the house and taking care of the yard. I imagined him having a regular job and contributing to the family resources, instead of draining our resources dry with his drinking. I thought about him going places with the family and our enjoying it. In my imaginary world there would be no fighting or arguing — just peace and tranquility. All of this was in my imagination, of course. Fiction. Pure fantasy. None of it was real. In reality my husband is a sick, old, angry, selfish, shriveled up shell-of-the-man-I-once-knew.

Whatever became of my prince in shining armor? I really couldn't tell you, because this time, *he* moved out.

All that I truly know, now, is that ever since he left, the atmosphere at home is more peaceful than it has ever been. The knockdown, dragged-out fights have vanished. I haven't had slept this restfully for years. I'm not lying awake all night wondering when, or if my husband will come home. There is more money in the bank for paying the utility bills and for buying food. The dramatic crisis situations are gone. Peace reigns over our household kingdom once again. It's been a long road…

But things aren't all rosy. The children miss their daddy. I miss him. I will admit; sometimes, it is lonely being a single parent. I wish I had an adult to talk to at nights. I want someone to lean on when things get rough at work, or when the kids drive me crazy. There is a void…

So, how can I fill that void – that empty feeling deep within my soul? I have found the answer to that question. Here it is:

Do not be anxious about anything, but in every situation, by prayer and petition, with thanksgiving, present your requests to God. And the peace of God, which transcends all understanding, will guard your hearts and your minds in Christ Jesus.

Finally, brothers and sisters, whatever is true, whatever is noble, whatever is right, whatever is pure, whatever is lovely, whatever is admirable—if anything is excellent or praiseworthy—think about such things. Philippians 4:6-8

The secret to filling the void of loneliness and uncertainty is to leave your burden at the foot of the cross, and stop snatching it back or telling

21 Finding Peace

God what to do with it. Completely separate yourself from the problem. Then, fill your mind with positive things like whatever is true, noble, right, pure, lovely, admirable, excellent and praiseworthy.

Come to me, all you who are weary and burdened, and I will give you rest. Take my yoke upon you and learn from me, for I am gentle and humble in heart, and you will find rest for your souls. For my yoke is easy and my burden is light. Matthew 11:28-30

In other words, let your mind dwell on positive things, not the dark foreboding things you're so used to focusing on in your alcoholic relationship.

You have dragged around that ball and chain of feeling responsible for your alcoholic's actions long enough. Cut the chain, give that iron ball of alcoholic to Jesus and be free! Don't think you are doing your alcoholic any favors by dragging his problems around with you. You aren't. When you release it, Jesus will give the ball of problems back to the alcoholic, who will drag it around until he figures out he needs to give it all over to Jesus – not to his wife, mother, pastor, or best friend.

Humbly bow before your creator. Pray for Him to take away the worry and your natural tendency to "fix things" for your alcoholic. Admit to God that your alcoholic has been your "drug of choice." You have made it your business to fix him. Thank Him for helping you realize that there is only One who can do the job of healing your alcoholic. Admit that all your efforts have availed nothing, and that you are ready to humbly lay the burden of alcoholism and everything that goes with it, down at the feet of Jesus.

God has been waiting for you here, at the cross, all along. His arms are opened wide. As you enter His embrace, He holds you tight and gently takes that heavy burden from your clinging hands. You reluctantly hand your alcoholic over to him, but as you do, you immediately notice a change. You are lighter. The pressure vanishes. What a relief! You are free! Praise God!

You dance and skip and twirl around at the sheer weightlessness you feel. Praise God!

You would think that praising God for taking your ball-and-chain of problems from you would come naturally, but sometimes it doesn't. Sometimes, it is hard to trust and believe that He really has taken it — that you don't need to be involved in solving your alcoholic's problems anymore. That is faith — a faith far beyond human comprehension.

How do I get this faith you ask? I love this story, because it can apply to an alcoholic just as easily. Read on. Here is your answer.

A man in the crowd answered, "Teacher, I brought you my son, who is possessed by a spirit that has robbed him of speech. Whenever it seizes him, it throws him to the ground. He foams at the mouth, gnashes his teeth and becomes rigid. I asked your disciples to drive out the spirit, but they could not."

"You unbelieving generation," Jesus replied, "how long shall I stay with you? How long shall I put up with you? Bring the boy to me."

So they brought him. When the spirit saw Jesus, it immediately threw the boy into a convulsion. He fell to the ground and rolled around, foaming at the mouth.

Jesus asked the boy's father, "How long has he been like this?"

"From childhood," he answered. "It has often thrown him into fire or water to kill him. But if you can do anything, take pity on us and help us."

"'If you can'?" said Jesus. "Everything is possible for one who believes."

Immediately the boy's father exclaimed, "I do believe; help me overcome my unbelief!"

When Jesus saw that a crowd was running to the scene, he rebuked the impure spirit. "You deaf and mute spirit," he said, "I command you, come out of him and never enter him again."

The spirit shrieked, convulsed him violently and came out. The boy looked so much like a corpse that many said, "He's dead." But Jesus took him by the hand and lifted him to his feet, and he stood up.

After Jesus had gone indoors, his disciples asked him privately, "Why couldn't we drive it out?"

He replied, "This kind can come out only by prayer." Mark 9:17-29

There it is. Pray a specific prayer to God. "I do believe; help me overcome my unbelief!"

That is all there is to it. If you pray for God to help you believe, He will take over the work to save your alcoholic and help you deal with the resulting problems of this disease. He will compassionately give you faith beyond human comprehension.

"But I have prayed and prayed and nothing has happened…"

21 Finding Peace

What? Your alcoholic is still drunk, you're still poor, and nothing has changed as far as you can tell? Well, let me share a little secret that God told me one day as I was going for a walk through the woods on our property.

And God said, "Stop. Look all around you. Be quiet and listen. What do you see? What do you hear? What is out there? What is going on around you?"

"Well, God, there are trees. I hear the wind and some birds chirping way up there in one of the treetops," I replied.

"What else do you see and hear?"

"Uh. Well, some birds on the ground are scratching. I hear some bees on the wild blueberry flowers. There are some tiny yellow and white flowers blooming down in the grass."

"What else?"

"I see all types of trees and bushes around me —lots of them. They are different shapes and sizes and colors. You know something God? There are a lot of things going on around here that I can't even see, hear, or smell, but that doesn't mean nothing is happening."

"That is exactly, my point. You look to your senses to know all that is going on in your alcoholic's life, but you really don't know it all. There is so much more that is going on that only I know about. I am working in a whole host of ways through people and circumstances that you don't know anything about. Only I do."

Oh, wow. I never thought of that.

So, there you have it. God is in control of everything. He thinks and knows of ways of influencing your alcoholic that you have no clue about. My only work is to trust Him and let Him speak and work through me in His own time and way.

What I'm saying is, "Just let that burden go, my brothers and sisters. Let it go!" Only then, will you be free, truly free, and at peace. Finally! Thank you, Jesus!

What is the burden you are carrying?

Part 3: Helping Yourself

What is keeping you from letting go of that burden?

God is moving in your alcoholic's life. Write some things you have seen God do.

21 Finding Peace

What would it take for you to give your alcoholic completely over to God?

Write a prayer asking for God to give you the strength needed to completely release your alcoholic over to him.

PART 4: RECOVERING FROM ALCOHOLISM

22 A DRY DRUNK

I will give them an undivided heart and put a new spirit in them; I will remove from them their heart of stone and give them a heart of flesh. Then they will follow my decrees and be careful to keep my laws. They will be my people, and I will be their God. Ezekiel 11:19-20

When I first began attending Al-Anon meetings, some of its members referred to their spouses as "dry drunks." I wondered what a dry drunk was. Later, I found out that a dry drunk is an alcoholic who is not actively drinking, not actively working a program of recovery, still exhibits the same old "stinkin' thinkin'," and still acts the same way he did when he was an active drunk.

There are three types of alcoholics — a drinking drunk, a dry drunk, or a sober man.

The drinking alcoholic is always in some stage of drunkenness. He is either planning on getting drunk, is drunk, or is going through the remorseful hangover stage that happens after a drunk. He is caught in Satan's vicious cycle of destruction through the use of the mind-altering drug, liquor. There are only five ways out of this dead-end cycle — jail, insanity, becoming a dry drunk, sobriety, or death. Of course, we all pray for sobriety, but unfortunately, this is not always the case.

The dry drunk, on the other hand, refrains from ingesting any type alcohol for long periods of time. This may mean weeks, months, or even years of abstinence. If his recovery involved a religious conversion, or a recovery program such as the one Alcoholics Anonymous offers, he is likely on the road to sobriety; however, be aware that the effects of the toxins he

22 A Dry Drunk

has been pouring into his body sometimes takes years to dissipate. So, expect that the chemical changes in his brain to take time to return to normal.

Dry drunks are usually the hardy, in your face, "manly men." They are easily "ticked off". Even though they may not be drinking, they will continue to exhibit alcoholic thinking and behaviors.

Often, you will hear a dry drunk say, "Look. I quit drinking like you wanted; so, quit @#^# at me!" He continues to be arrogant, selfish, controlling, manipulating and critical to those around him. He still hangs around the same bad influences, and acts the same way he did while he was drinking.

The only good thing I can say about dry drunks is that at least their bodies are getting a much-needed vacation from the constant flush of toxins.

What everyone hopes and prays for is true sobriety. A sober alcoholic will regularly attend AA meetings, or has undergone a true religious conversion.

Interestingly, the 12 steps of AA closely follow the Biblical principles of conversion. Take a close look at the steps outlined in AA's recovery program.

THE TWELVE STEPS OF ALCOHOLICS ANONYMOUS

1. We admitted we were powerless over alcohol—that our lives had become unmanageable.

2. Came to believe that a Power greater than ourselves could restore us to sanity.

3. Made a decision to turn our will and our lives over to the care of God as we understood Him.

4. Made a searching and fearless moral inventory of ourselves.

5. Admitted to God, to ourselves, and to another human being the exact nature of our wrongs.

Part 4: Recovering from Alcoholism

6. Were entirely ready to have God remove all these defects of character.

7. Humbly asked Him to remove our shortcomings.

8. Made a list of all persons we had harmed, and became willing to make amends to them all.

9. Made direct amends to such people wherever possible, except when to do so would injure them or others.

10. Continued to take personal inventory and when we were wrong promptly admitted it.

11. Sought through prayer and meditation to improve our conscious contact with God, as we understood Him, praying only for knowledge of His will for us and the power to carry that out.

12. Having had a spiritual awakening as the result of these Steps, we tried to carry this message to alcoholics, and to practice these principles in all our affairs.

_{The Twelve Steps are reprinted with permission of Alcoholics Anonymous World Services, Inc. ("AAWS") Permission to reprint the Twelve Steps does not mean that AAWS has reviewed or approved the contents of this publication, or that AAWS necessarily agrees with the views expressed herein. A.A. is a program of recovery from alcoholism only - use of the Twelve Steps in connection with programs and activities which are patterned after A.A., but which address other problems, or in any other non-A.A. context, does not imply otherwise. Additionally, while A.A. is a spiritual program, A.A. is not a religious program. Thus, A.A. is not affiliated or allied with any sect, denomination, or specific religious belief.}

I find the similarity between the process of a Christian's conversion and AA's 12 steps to be astonishingly parallel. This is why a religious experience can work the same as working the twelve steps.

This also explains why you occasionally hear success stories about church members who work tirelessly with an alcoholic who eventually becomes sober. This spiritual conversion is a witness to devout leadership, the power of prayer, and the working of the Holy Spirit. Praise the Lord for

22 A Dry Drunk

faithful church shepherds who care enough to take the time and effort to lead the lost back to the fold.

One other thing I'd like to mention on this subject. If you are separated or divorced from an alcoholic and wish to reconcile safely and successfully, don't fall for the, "Well, I'm not drinking, now; so, let's get back together" lure.

Prayerfully examine the situation first. If he is still blaming you for the relationship problems, still wanting to pick fights and argue, still making excuses for his adultery while under the influence, still going into rages for all kinds of crazy things, acting in totally irrational ways, still hanging out with his same old drinking buddies, still not showing an interest in the family, still not making a living or going to church with the rest of the family, it's a pretty sure thing that you are dealing with a dry drunk. Don't look for things to improve. They won't. You will continue to have the same old marriage problems. Only now, they will be exaggerated, because you won't have the drinking to blame. This kind of situation would not be wise to go back into.

However, if your alcoholic is working a recovery program or had a religious experience and is really sober, you will see a marked difference in his personality. He will be humble, kind, admit his faults, will work to follow God's bidding, will go to church with his family, will be transparently open and honest in all that he does, will work to restore trust and respect, will be slow to anger, and will do his best to restore financial security for his family. This is the personality of a sober man. That's what you are praying for.

This will not all happen over night. It will take time, effort, prayer and commitment on the alcoholic's part. If he is faithful, God will transform his stony heart into a heart of flesh.

Returning to a converted man will be a rewarding and successful experience. Joyfully, come back together – praising the Lord for his saving power.

What is a "drinking alcoholic"?

Part 4: Recovering from Alcoholism

What is a "dry drunk"?

How can you know if an alcoholic is truly sober?

How is your alcoholic acting?

22 A Dry Drunk

Which of the three types of alcoholics is your loved one?

23 DETOX AND REHAB

As a result, they do not live the rest of their earthly lives for evil human desires, but rather for the will of God. For you have spent enough time in the past doing what pagans choose to do—living in debauchery, lust, drunkenness, orgies, carousing and detestable idolatry. 1 Peter 4:2, 3

"He's in detox!" I sent this e-mail message to many of my friends and family when my husband went into detox. I was ecstatic. I was certain the Lord was working, and that my husband would soon be free from his alcoholism. Everything would get back to normal in our family and love would reign supreme. Well, I was right in that the Lord was working, but not in the ways that I thought.

This is how he made the decision to go to detox.

He staggered in around 1 A.M. after a day, evening, and night of heavy drinking. In the morning he had the mother of all hangovers. The remorse, sorrow, and hopelessness were very real to him. He begged me to stay home from work to be with him. He didn't feel he could make it through the day alone. He said he wanted to quit drinking and hated what it was doing to him and his family.

I, as naive as I was about "hangover remorse," figured, "Hey, maybe he's ready to go to rehab." I told him that the only way he was going to be able to quit would be to go to detox. He agreed. I was shocked.

I felt I had better work quickly – before he changed his mind. I tried to get off from work, but couldn't find anyone to fill in for me; so, I called my husband's best friend, a sober for 25 years alcoholic, to come stay with him. I called the local detox center on my way to work and with many phone

23 Detox and Rehab

calls back and forth with my husband's friend and the detox center made all the arrangements for him to go.

All this took time and as the hangover began to wear off during the day, so did my husband's resolve to go. He began to say he felt better, and that he could quit on his own, he couldn't just up and leave his work, he had things to do, he didn't have the money to pay for rehab, etc. – **all** the usual excuses not to go.

I keep using "detox" and "rehab" interchangeably on purpose, because I thought they were one and the same at the time. Now, I know differently.

He finally did enter detox at 5 P.M. that evening, but not until he let us know that he wasn't so sure he was doing the right thing. I didn't care what he said, as long as he went. I figured they would wave their magic wands there and as long as he did what they said, he'd be cured. I was so happy and thankful to God. He was in.

While at detox they had family visiting hours and meetings I could attend. I went to these religiously — eager to do anything and everything they said, if it would make even the smallest difference. The first meeting was great. My husband made googley eyes at me and held my hand during the meeting. I thought this was great until I found out later he was flying high on Valium as they brought him down from his alcohol and Xanax addictions. I smile as I remember the feelings I had. I was finally loved and appreciated by him so much that he finally wanted to change. Now, everything was changing for the better. I patted myself on the back.

Not...

The next meeting, when I went to visit him at the detox center, things went totally opposite; my husband was demanding and anxious. He wanted to make sure I was doing everything at home to his precise specifications, and of course, I wasn't — not to his expectations. He was also upset that I didn't show him enough attention while I was there. He said I seemed like I wanted to leave. Well, yeah! I didn't go in there to be attacked! Anyway, I found out later that he was detoxing with little or no drugs at that point, and his body was screaming for some type of medication; thus, the edginess and anxiety. He was being perfectly normal for where he was in the process of detoxification.

I had so much to learn!

Part 4: Recovering from Alcoholism

The bad news is that after 8 days, he called me and said he was coming home and to come pick him up. He stated that he felt better and had things he had to do at work. There was just no way he could stay in treatment. I called his nurse after I got off the phone with him, and she informed me that he was being released against the doctor's orders. He was not ready to go, but they couldn't keep him against his will.

I, being the "good wife" that I was, just hurried my little self over to the rehab center to pick him up. Was he appreciative? Of course not!

"What took you so long...." Truth be told I didn't want to come and get him at all. I did take my time in going to pick him up. I was hoping it would close before I got there. I guess that kind of backfired. Didn't it?

He went to AA meetings at least once a day for about a week, then it began to be fewer and fewer times. Needless to say, he was drinking and drugging again after only about 2 weeks.

I was devastated. How could he be back to drinking again so soon?

I scoured the Internet for clues. Did this happen often? Was he a rare case to go back to drinking so soon after leaving "rehab?"

What I found out was that my husband was in "detox," not "rehab." The detoxification center's job was to bring him down gently from the drugs. They also tried to begin the education on what alcohol and drugs do to your body and start him down the path to sobriety. In reality, detox is only the tip of the iceberg in recovery.

Now, I've learned that after detox comes rehab. Rehabilitation is usually anywhere from 30 days to a year after they successfully complete detox. They can be an inpatient or outpatient, depending on the circumstances and severity of the addictions. Most all rehabs include attending Alcoholics Anonymous and completing the 12 steps as part of their program. Some are religious based programs. Either way, rehab is an essential part of recovery.

My husband has been to detox twice. He checked himself out early each time and the drinking continued. He made it 29 days before drinking the second time.

I guess the moral of the story is that unless your loved one goes into detox or rehab because he wants to quit drinking, not for your sake or to keep the peace, you are pretty much wasting your time and money. This is

23 Detox and Rehab

from my experience and from talking with others in similar situations. There may be an extremely small percentage that actually get sober when "forced to" or "talked into" checking into a program via an intervention.

I believe that in the vast majority of cases, the alcoholic has to come to a point in his life where he sees that the life his is living is not the best for him. He is not as happy as he thought he would be. Things aren't working out as planned... He is poor, destitute, sick, and tired. He comes to the place where he is sick and tired of being sick and tired — a.k.a. "rock bottom." The want for change has to come from within the alcoholic, or all the programs in the world will not do a bit of good.

So, why did I say God was working in all this? Because, I believe the whole thing was a journey for me to realize that I could not and would never be able to fix my husband's problems. This process is between God and him. What a long lesson this has been for me. I am still learning to "let go and let God," as they say in AA.

What is the difference between detox and rehab?

24 THE LOST SON RETURNS

I tell you that in the same way there will be more rejoicing in heaven over one sinner who repents than over ninety-nine righteous persons who do not need to repent. Luke 15:7

Have you ever wondered, "What is it going to take for my alcoholic to become sober? What will it take for him to hit his 'rock bottom?' When will he come to his senses?" I know I have.

Well, if you look closely at a Biblical account of Jesus' parable of "The Lost Son," you will see what it will take for most alcoholics to come to their senses. Let's read the story carefully — looking for clues.

Jesus continued: "There was a man who had two sons. The younger one said to his father, 'Father, give me my share of the estate.' So he divided his property between them.

"Not long after that, the younger son got together all he had, set off for a distant country and there squandered his wealth in wild living.

"After he had spent everything, there was a severe famine in that whole country, and he began to be in need. So he went and hired himself out to a citizen of that country, who sent him to his fields to feed pigs. He longed to fill his stomach with the pods that the pigs were eating, but no one gave him anything.

"When he came to his senses, he said, 'How many of my father's hired servants have food to spare, and here I am starving to death! I will set out and go back to my father and say to him: Father, I have sinned against heaven and against you. I am no longer worthy to be called your son; make me like one of your hired servants.' So he got up and went to his father."

24 The Lost Son Returns

"But while he was still a long way off, his father saw him and was filled with compassion for him; he ran to his son, threw his arms around him and kissed him.

"The son said to him, 'Father, I have sinned against heaven and against you. I am no longer worthy to be called your son.'

"But the father said to his servants, 'Quick! Bring the best robe and put it on him. Put a ring on his finger and sandals on his feet. Bring the fattened calf and kill it. Let's have a feast and celebrate. For this son of mine was dead and is alive again; he was lost and is found.' So they began to celebrate." Luke 15:11-24

I'd like to point out several amazing aspects involved in this story.

First, isn't it amazing how the father gave the youngest son what he wanted? He didn't plead with him to reconsider, but instead granted him his request without questioning his intentions. He fully knew the terrible disasters, which could happen to his son as a result of his foolish request. God is like that. He sorrowfully allows us to make our own decisions even though they may lead to our own destruction.

Let's look closely at the factors it took to bring this young man to his senses.

"After he had spent everything, there was a severe famine in that whole country, and he began to be in need. So he went and hired himself out to a citizen of that country, who sent him to his fields to feed pigs. He longed to fill his stomach with the pods that the pigs were eating, but no one gave him anything."

First, he wasted away his money on his riotous living. He got to the point where he was utterly and completely broke. *"He began to be in need."* At this point his rich father could have rented him an apartment, given him a job, or loaned him some money to get through the rough times, but he didn't. He didn't go after him and try to rescue him from his folly. He left him to see the natural consequences of his behavior.

It got to the point where he was hungry and desperate for food, but "no one gave him anything." In fact, he was willing to take any job available to put food in his mouth. This is key.

It may seem on the surface cruel that no one helped him out of his predicament, but in reality, the alcoholic has to get to this point, before he sees his need for redemption. If he has someone to rescue him at every turn, his sickness will continue its progression toward death. He needs to be allowed the dignity of working himself out of the results of his behavior.

As a result of these natural consequences, he is able to see things as they really are for the first time. He begins to remember what he has given up — people who really love him and belonging to a family that cares. He begins to think, "Oh, what have I done?!"

Then, something amazing happens. He decides to make amends with his family. This is a sign of true surrender on his part. He is ready to make things right with God and his family. Let's look again at those verses.

"When he came to his senses, he said, 'How many of my father's hired servants have food to spare, and here I am starving to death! I will set out and go back to my father and say to him: Father, I have sinned against heaven and against you. I am no longer worthy to be called your son; make me like one of your hired servants.' So he got up and went to his father.

"But while he was still a long way off, his father saw him and was filled with compassion for him; he ran to his son, threw his arms around him and kissed him.

"The son said to him, 'Father, I have sinned against heaven and against you. I am no longer worthy to be called your son.'"

The son followed through with his plans for amends with God and his family, "Father, I have sinned against heaven and against you. I am no longer worthy to called your son." This type of humility is what is needed for true repentance.

Not until you see this kind of humility from your alcoholic can you really expect to see any real changes in his lifestyle. If you do, then praise the Lord. He is truly on his way to recovery, and if this is the case, feel free to celebrate and throw a party with your family. Welcome him home with open arms, hugs and kisses. The old is passed away, and he is on his way to becoming a new creature.

There are so many truths for successfully living out our lives today in the Bible. These stories are there for a reason. We should carefully study and reap the benefits of the accounts, stories, and wisdom the Bible has to offer. God is good.

24 The Lost Son Returns

Have you allowed your alcoholic the freedom to reap the consequences of his actions? How?

If not, what can you do to quit "fixing" everything for your alcoholic?

What are some things you do to "check up on" your alcoholic?

Has this helped him make the decision to quit drinking? Why not?

To be like the father in this story, you must leave the alcoholic alone to face his own consequences to his behavior. What can you do to make this possible?

How will you welcome home your "lost son?"

25 RECOVERY

Therefore, my dear brothers, stand firm. Let nothing move you. Always give yourselves fully to the work of the Lord, because you know that your labor in the Lord is not in vain. 1 Corinthians 15:58

"Yippee! My alcoholic is finally really sober!"

It's been a long hard road, and you can't believe it's finally over. Well, it's a fabulous turn of events, but be careful. The journey to recovery is not over just yet.

There are two things you need to focus on. Keep your focus where it needs to be — on you not him. He needs to work out his own recovery, and you need to focus on your recovery.

First, there is no guarantee that he will remain sober, or that the relationship will be "happily ever after." Though his sobriety may be short lived, you can't live like he's still drinking. You have to settle it in your mind that, as of right now, he is sober. It is what it is.

Fear of his returning to alcoholism can cause more problems in the relationship. If you nag him to keep going to his AA meetings, going to church, and reading his Big Book, it will only cause more contention in your marriage. Keep in mind that his journey to sobriety is his journey and not yours. Leave him be. You have enough to worry about as far as your journey to recovery.

Your journey to recovery continues by you asking yourself whether you have recovered from your sickness? Your sickness has been that you have been addicted to healing someone that doesn't want to be healed. You have had a lot to learn — how to set boundaries, how to be honest, kind, patient, and considerate — yet firm. You've had to learn how to rely on God and yourself for your happiness.

Instead of focusing on how well your alcoholic's sobriety is coming, focus on your recovery. Honestly ask yourself, "Do I display all the 'fruits of the Spirit'?" If you don't, then there is more work to be done. Remember, this is a daily task you will need to do. Go before God daily seeking His direction, and humbly accepting his leading.

But the fruit of the Spirit is love, joy, peace, patience, kindness, goodness, faithfulness, gentleness and self-control. Against such things there is no law. Galatians 5:22, 23

These new qualities in you are going to be just as essential in making your renewed relationship successful, as your alcoholic's sobriety will. You are just as responsible for fixing these flaws in your personality, as he is responsible for his recovery. Without this mutual healing, a successful and happy marriage is next to impossible.

A lot of times we have the false notion that once "they get sober" all is going to be peaches and cream and blueberry cobbler. There will be long romantic walks on the beach holding hands and whispering sweet nothings, and all your dreams will come true. Ha! In your dreams...

The problems you had before he started drinking will still be there. If you hated the way he threw his underwear on the floor before, look for it to still be there now. If he hated visiting your mother then, he will most likely still hate visiting her. The problems, that were never resolved before the drinking began, are still there.

Before, when problems arose. You were to blame. That's what he said, and that's what you believed. Now, in sobriety, things will be different in that you will be able to talk things over. Discuss things that you were afraid to discuss in the past. Things that were swept under the rug so to speak; yet, kept coming up over and over again... You will be able to speak about these things openly and honestly and be able to come up with solutions on a common ground. Essentially, you will be playing "grownup."

25 Recovery

Sobriety is not a cure all. It is a new way of handling problems. It is being patient and understanding of each other's needs and being willing to sacrifice your own wants and needs for your alcoholic's.

That will be such a delight. I am looking forward to that day. We have not reached this level in our relationship, but I hear it's true, and it happens. I believe it will happen for me someday. I pray for it, look forward to it, and in the mean time I continue to work on fixing myself.

Define sobriety?

What are your ideas on what sobriety will look like in your home?

Why is it just as necessary for you to continue to work a program of recovery as it is for your alcoholic?

Which fruits of the Spirit do your alcoholic display?

Which fruits of the Spirit do you display?

Write some ways you can you uplift your alcoholic?

25 Recovery

You will need to experience a daily walk with the Lord in order for sobriety to stick. Devise a plan for your daily meditation time with God.

PART 5: MOVING FORWARD

Part 5: Moving Forward

26 RECONCILIATION

They claim to know God, but by their actions they deny him. They are detestable, disobedient and unfit for doing anything good. Titus 1:16

If you have already separated from or divorced your alcoholic, you may eventually be faced with the decision as to whether or not it would be beneficial to reconcile. This can be a hard decision, but there are some things to look for in order to help predict whether your reunion will be successful or a disaster.

Actions speak louder than words in this case. Your alcoholic may tell you he loves you and is sorry for what he has done and wants to change. Really? Talk is cheap. Actions are what will reveal the real story.

Here are some indicators to look for that show he is serious about his recovery.

- He regularly attends AA without you saying a word.
- He puts his recovery ahead of his work and family. I know this sounds wrong, but it really isn't. It is the only way he can recover.
- He puts God first in his life.
- You see him studying God's word daily on his own.
- He goes to church without nagging.
- He avoids arguments.
- He is humbly admits when he makes a mistake.
- He is grateful you held out in their marriage and gave him another chance.

26 Reconciliation

- He regularly makes amends. You should see a big change in this area.
- He openly and eagerly shares where he is going and calls in when he is going to be late.
- He no longer hides his cell phone messages and history from you.
- If he "falls off the wagon" he tells you right away and doubles his efforts toward sobriety.
- He seeks to support his family financially.
- He humbly works hard to regain the love and respect he lost.
- He no longer hangs out with his old drinking buddies.

If the above behaviors are the ones you are observing, then God be praised! Your alcoholic has a very good chance of staying sober and in recovery. Continue to support him in his recovery and daily pray with him as a couple.

If you don't see these types of behaviors, beware. He is probably not in recovery.

Here are some "red flags" to watch for. If his recovery is not genuine, you will observe these types of behaviors.

- He starts making excuses to not attend AA meetings.
- He becomes too busy for personal devotions.
- He drops you and the kids off at church or stays home, because he doesn't feel good or has other obligations that have to be met.
- He becomes irritable and flies off the handle at little annoyances.
- He is arrogant.
- He specializes in pity parties. Poor me. Nothing is going right for him. Waaa waaa waaa.
- He holds a lot of resentment towards others.
- He blames others for his situation.
- He starts to hang out with his old drinking buddies again.
- He starts showing up late. You don't know where he has been, and he doesn't appreciate you nagging him about it.

- He makes up excuses why he can't go to work.
- He doesn't care to talk about his recovery.
- He demands respect from the children and you.
- He wants to leave detox or rehab early against doctors orders.

If this is what you are seeing, he will most likely go back to drinking sooner or later — most likely sooner. A white-knuckling dry drunk can't hang on long without a drink. More than likely, he will return to his own ways within one year.

Sadly, I have learned these signs through experience. No matter how much I wish for it to be a certain way, it is what it is. I have to learn to accept reality and work with what I have — not what I wish I had.

Look at these signs for indicators as to whether the time is right for reconciliation or not. There is no rush. Don't be too hasty about getting back together. If he is not ready, don't rush into anything.

Prayerfully ask God for guidance in this matter. He will guide you if you ask. You will know without a doubt what to do. It will feel right in your gut. That is His still small voice directing you to the right path.

Trust in the LORD with all your heart and lean not on your own understanding; in all your ways acknowledge him, and he will make your paths straight. Proverbs 3:5, 6

If you do make a mistake and get back together before the time is right, don't stress it. You can always move back out. We all make mistakes. Allow your Father in Heaven to bear you up in his arms. He is always ready and waiting to listen and lead.

If you are separated or divorced, what changes would you need to see in order for you to go back to your alcoholic?

26 Reconciliation

What is your alcoholic saying to you?

What are his actions saying to you?

What is that still small voice saying to you?

Part 5: Moving Forward

27 DECISIONS

Hope in the LORD and keep his way. He will exalt you to inherit the land; when the wicked are destroyed, you will see it. Psalms 37:34

Making the right decision at the right time is not always possible. Yes, we all make mistakes, but sometimes making no decision is worse than making a mistake. Not making any decision means that you are standing still – stagnant.

As co-dependents we are so afraid of making a mistake. We fear the wrath of the alcoholic. We fear his leaving, his violence, his rejection, and abandonment. We fear. We fear. We fear; therefore nothing happens. Nothing changes. We remain in the same mess we have always been in and wonder why things aren't getting better.

In her 1983 book, <u>Sudden Death</u>, Rita Mae Brown wrote on page 68, "Insanity is doing the same thing over and over again but expecting different results."

Yes, that's us all right. We keep praying for things to change, but we don't move forward. We just sit around at home all alone in our private little pity party crying out to Him, "Why does it always happen to me. Bring me some relief, God!

There is a way that seems right to a man, but in the end it leads to death. Proverbs 14:12

Thankfully, God does send relief and give us direction. The problem is, many times, we either don't see it, or are not ready to accept it. Our eyes are glued on the path we are used to taking. We feel comfortable there. We know the route. We don't want to leave the road. It's the obvious way to go.

Is it really?

God isn't in the business of picking us up and placing us where we need to be. He gives us the wisdom we need to know. He tells us which way to go, and then it's our job to make those changes happen.

There are road signs along the path of life that we need to pay attention to. There are signs of pain, signs of counsel, signs of promises, signs of clues, and signs of impressions. If we follow these signs we can be sure we are doing the right thing. We will feel at peace with the World and ourselves.

The sign of pain is telling us that change needs to be made. If you are in physical pain, your body is telling you something is wrong. You need to go to the doctor and get a diagnosis to find out what part of your body is not functioning properly and get it cut it out or fixed. You may be feeling the physical pain of a stomach ulcer, headaches, or tension neck pain. Maybe, it's emotional pain you are feeling. Either way, you need to find out what is causing it. Pinpoint it. Be very specific. Then see what you can do about fixing that problem or getting rid of the problem all together.

The sign of counsel is one that usually has to be sought out. Look for Godly counsel from your Bible, pastor, parents, books, websites, or a counselor that specializes in alcoholism. Then listen and learn. Hopefully, they have had years of learned knowledge, experience, and God-given wisdom. They will give you ideas, you may have never thought of before. Be open to their advice.

The sign of promises comes from the Bible. God promises to be with us and guide our steps. Lean on Him. Search the scriptures with all your heart, and he will show you what to do.

O people of Zion, who live in Jerusalem, you will weep no more. How gracious he will be when you cry for help! As soon as he hears, he will answer you. Although the Lord gives you the bread of adversity and the water of affliction, your teachers will be hidden no more; with your own eyes you will see them. Whether you turn to the right or to the left, your ears will hear a voice behind you, saying, 'This is the way; walk in it.'" Isaiah 30:19-21

The clue sign is a bright neon orange sign that is about 20 feet in diameter, smack dab in the center of the highway.

You've heard the phrase, "Get a clue!" That's what you need to do. If you don't have money, get a job. If your husband hits you every time he comes home drunk, don't be there when he gets home. If your child throws up green beans every time you feed it to him, don't feed him green beans anymore. Maybe asparagus will do... If the sign is so obvious, why do you keep inching our way around it? Pretending like it is not there?!

Because you're afraid to look at it. Stop. Face it. Touch it. Think about it. Cry over it, because it's not going anywhere, and you can't move it.

So, what are you going to do about it? Quit being a wimp, and don God's armor. Face that bad boy head on. Smash your proverbial car straight into it and run over it. Okay. Okay. I think you get the picture...

Such confidence as this is ours through Christ before God. Not that we are competent in ourselves to claim anything for ourselves, but our competence comes from God. He has made us competent... 2 Corinthians 3: 4-6

It's easy to miss the sign of impressions. It is often this misty sign next to the road, hiding behind a tree. It moves and becomes clear one minute and vanishes the next. If you are not looking for it, you won't see it. It is the voice of Holy Spirit. He is the great Counselor that the Lord has sent to guide and direct you and me. Pray to God to send you an answer through the voice of the Holy Spirit. Stop and take time to listen for it. Don't just pray and sit around the house. Get up, and go about your business. Remain in prayer however, waiting for God to talk to you. He will let you know, but it won't be anything loud or earth shattering. It will be a quite soft urging in your soul. You will be impressed what to do. It's in your gut. It will be the right thing, and you will know it – without a shadow of a doubt. If you dedicate your life to the Lord every day and seek his guidance He will not let you down.

The Biblical story of Elijah tells about a time he was discouraged. Read his account of when God talked to him. Elijah begins with telling God all about his problem. Then he waits for God to answer. Read what happens.

"...I am the only one left, and now they are trying to kill me too."

27 Decisions

The Lord said, "Go out and stand on the mountain in the presence of the Lord, for the Lord is about to pass by."

Then a great and powerful wind tore the mountains apart and shattered the rocks before the Lord, but the Lord was not in the wind. After the wind there was an earthquake, but the Lord was not in the earthquake. After the earthquake came a fire, but the Lord was not in the fire. And after the fire came a gentle whisper.

When Elijah heard it, he pulled his cloak over his face and went out and stood at the mouth of the cave.

Then a voice said to him, "What are you doing here, Elijah?" 1 Kings 19: 10-13

God will talk to you in the same soft gentle whisper. Listen and know. If you make a decision to do something, and it just doesn't seem right with your intuition, it isn't. If you ask God to guide you, he will. It will feel right. You will know it. You will be at peace with your decision.

One other thing I'd like to caution you about is getting too comfortable on the road you're on. Just because you know the road well, doesn't mean it's the right road.

If you find that everybody and their brother is on the same road, this doesn't mean that it is the right road for you. You will need to do the work of deciding whether it is right for you or not.

Watch for the signs, and let them direct you.

Who knows, you may become the next Lewis and Clark – forging new roads and discovering knew places more spectacular than you ever imagined.

Happy discovering!

List some decisions you feel you need to make.

Part 5: Moving Forward

What are some signs that you see regarding that decision?

Are your "signs" in accordance with scriptures? If so, move prayerfully forward. If not, then you need to leave that sign alone. It is not from the Lord. List things you need to leave behind as your alcoholic comes to grips with the disease.

28 LETTING GO

Humble yourselves, therefore, under God's mighty hand, that he may lift you up in due time. Cast all your anxiety on him because he cares for you. 1 Peter 5: 6,7

This book has been about understanding, helping, healing, and making changes in your lives.

You have come to a better understanding of your alcoholic. He isn't the big man he makes himself out to be. His arrogance is a sham, and he knows it. His brain is unable to make moral decisions. He has come to love only himself and his booze.

We've discussed his healing and your healing. Learning that we cannot change an alcoholic. The alcoholic will have to make his own decision, in his own time, and work a program of recovery. Your healing is all that you are in control of. That is a change that you can make.

We may hope and pray that our beloved alcoholic will get sober, will give his life to God, come home to our family, and come to his senses before his body completely shuts down. Sadly, this will not happen in most cases, and is something we need to talk about.

God is a god of love. He does not force anyone to love him or to give his life over to him. He loves him and chases after him, not wanting to let go. He doesn't quit his pursuit as long as there is a shred of hope left for his conversion. He is a Father with a passion for His children.

Unfortunately, some alcoholics never hit bottom until that bottom is the grave. Sometimes, he dies a broken man without a family, a home, not a penny to his name, or a relationship with God. He has turned a deaf ear to God for so long that the Holy Spirit has finally whispered His last, and has sadly left him alone in his misery. This does happen.

How can we know when there is no more hope for the relationship? I think that we will just know. God will no longer lay that burden on our heart to pray earnestly for him. There will be the peace of acceptance in our heart in knowing that we have done all we could. It is finished. It is over.

In all their distress he too was distressed, and the angel of his presence saved them. In his love and mercy he redeemed them; he lifted them up and carried them all the days of old. Yet they rebelled and grieved his Holy Spirit. So he turned and became their enemy and he himself fought against them. Isaiah 63: 9,10

I know I prayed for years and years for a happy marriage with my husband. I couldn't figure out why God wasn't answering my prayers. I finally learned there are some prayers God can't answer. Those are the one that involve people. People have to make up their own minds. He has given them that choice. He will not force anyone into heaven. And when I came to realize that, it became clear that I could never have a happy marriage with someone that had chosen to turn from God, his family, and all that is good. I had to accept that was the way it was.

People are people. My alcoholic husband is who he is, and I don't have any control over his decisions. I had to finally let it all go, and let God take everything. I had to accept that the fight for our relationship was over, and there was no future for us.

He has chosen his master, and my daughters and I have chosen ours.

My alcoholic husband filed for divorce. I knew it was time. God bids us not be unequally yoked with unbelievers, as a house divided cannot stand.

Do not be joined to unbelievers. What do right and wrong have in common? Can light and darkness be friends? How can Christ and Satan agree? What does a believer have in common with an unbeliever? 2 Corinthians 6:14, 15

But! If you are still waking up in the middle of the night and hearing God telling you to pray for him, then, by all means, keep praying. If you see little sparks of light of change in your alcoholic, then you can know — not to give up on him yet. If he shows the slightest interest in change for the good, know that the Holy Spirit is still at work.

28 Letting Go

Keep on praying. Keep lifting him up to God in prayer. You may be his only lifeline to heaven.

I know that God loves you and wants what's best for you. I also know he loves your alcoholic and wants what's best for him. He can see the end from the beginning. Give it to God to figure out. Put your alcoholic relationship in His hands and accept God's leading in your lives. Finally, you can be happy and at peace. May God go with you in your journey.

List some things you have come to understand about your alcoholic.

List some things you have learned about how you handle an alcoholic relationship.

Part 5: Moving Forward

What is God telling you to do about your alcoholic relationship?

What are you willing to do about your alcoholic relationship?

28 Letting Go

How can you make up the difference in what God is telling you to do, and what you are willing to do with your alcoholic relationship?

APPENDIX A: BIBLICAL QUOTES

Promises of Encouragement

You may ask me for anything in my name, and I will do it. John 14:14

Whoever serves me must follow me; and where I am, my servant also will be. My Father will honor the one who serves me. John 12:26

Then my head will be exalted above the enemies who surround me; at his tabernacle will I sacrifice with shouts of joy; I will sing and make music to the Lord. Psalm 27:6

Every good and perfect gift is from above, coming down from the Father of the heavenly lights, who does not change like shifting shadows. James 1:17

Therefore I tell you, whatever you ask for in prayer, believe that you have received it, and it will be yours. Mark 11:24

So I say to you: Ask and it will be given to you; seek and you will find; knock and the door will be opened to you. Luke 11:9

Again, I tell you that if two of you on earth agree about anything you ask for, it will be done for you by my Father in heaven. Matt. 18:19

As for me, far be it from me that I should sin against the Lord by failing to pray for you. And I will teach you the way that is good and right. 1 Samuel 12:23

If you believe, you will receive whatever you ask for in prayer. Matt. 21:22

Do not be anxious about anything, but in everything, by prayer and petition, with thanksgiving, present your requests to God. And the peace of

Appendix A: Biblical Quotes

God, which transcends all understanding, will guard your hearts and your minds in Christ Jesus. Philippians 4:6-7

Jesus answered them, "It is not the healthy who need a doctor, but the sick. I have not come to call the righteous, but sinners to repentance." Luke 5:31, 32

If he sins against you seven times in a day, and seven times comes back to you and says, 'I repent,' forgive him. Luke 17:4

Trust in the Lord and do good; dwell in the land and enjoy safe pasture. Delight yourself in the Lord and he will give you the desires of your heart. Psalm 37:3, 4

Verses on Drunkenness

Like a thorn bush in a drunkard's hand is a proverb in the mouth of a fool. Proverbs 26:9

The Lord has poured into them a spirit of dizziness; they make Egypt stagger in all that she does, as a drunkard staggers around in his vomit. Isaiah 19:14

Wake up, you drunkards, and weep! Wail, all you drinkers of wine; wail because of the new wine, for it has been snatched from your lips. Joel 1:5

But now I am writing you that you must not associate with anyone who calls himself a brother but is sexually immoral or greedy, an idolater or a slanderer, a drunkard or a swindler. With such a man do not even eat. 1 Corinthians 5:11

Do you not know that the wicked will not inherit the kingdom of God? Do not be deceived: Neither the sexually immoral nor idolaters nor adulterers nor male prostitutes nor homosexual offenders nor thieves nor the greedy nor drunkards nor slanderers nor swindlers will inherit the kingdom of God. And that is what some of you were. But you were washed, you were sanctified, you were justified in the name of the Lord Jesus Christ and by the Spirit of our God. 1 Corinthians 6:9-11

Wine is a mocker and beer a brawler; whoever is led astray by them is not wise. Proverbs 20:1

Listen, my son, and be wise, and keep your heart on the right path. Do not join those who drink too much wine or gorge themselves on meat, for drunkards and gluttons become poor, and drowsiness clothes them in rags. Proverbs 23:19-21

Who has woe? Who has sorrow? Who has strife? Who has complaints? Who has needless bruises? Who has bloodshot eyes? Those who linger over wine, who go to sample bowls of mixed wine. Do not gaze at wine when it is red, when it sparkles in the cup, when it goes down smoothly! In the end it bites like a snake and poisons like a viper. Proverbs 23: 29-32

It is not for kings, O Lemuel— not for kings to drink wine, not for rulers to crave beer lest they drink and forget what the law decrees, and deprive all the oppressed of their rights. Proverbs 31:4, 5

Woe to those who rise early in the morning to run after their drinks, who stay up late at night 'till they are inflamed with wine. They have harps and lyres at their banquets, tambourines and flutes and wine, but they have no regard for the deeds of the Lord, no respect for the work of his hands. Isaiah 5:11, 12

Woe to those who are heroes at drinking wine and champions at mixing drinks, Isaiah 5:22

Woe to that wreath, the pride of Ephraim's drunkards, to the fading flower, his glorious beauty, set on the head of a fertile valley— to that city, the pride of those laid low by wine! See, the Lord has one who is powerful and strong. Like a hailstorm and a destructive wind, like a driving rain and a

Appendix A: Biblical Quotes

flooding downpour, he will throw it forcefully to the ground. That wreath, the pride of Ephraim's drunkards, will be trampled underfoot. Isaiah 28:1-3

And these also stagger from wine and reel from beer: Priests and prophets stagger from beer and are befuddled with wine; they reel from beer, they stagger when seeing visions, they stumble when rendering decisions. All the tables are covered with vomit and there is not a spot without filth. Isaiah 28:7, 8

But they replied, "We do not drink wine, because our forefather Jonadab son of Recab gave us this command: neither you nor your descendants must ever drink wine." Jeremiah 35:6

They will eat but not have enough; they will engage in prostitution but not increase, because they have deserted the Lord to give themselves to prostitution, to old wine and new, which take away the understanding of my people. They consult a wooden idol and are answered by a stick of wood. A spirit of prostitution leads them astray; they are unfaithful to their God. Hosea 4:10-12

Whatever they plot against the Lord he will bring to an end; trouble will not come a second time. They will be entangled among thorns and drunk from their wine; they will be consumed like dry stubble. Nahum 1:9-1

See, he is puffed up; his desires are not upright - but the righteous will live by his faith — indeed, wine betrays him; he is arrogant and never at rest. Because he is as greedy as the grave and like death is never satisfied, he gathers to himself all the nations and takes captive all the peoples. Habakkuk 2:4, 5

Woe to him who gives drink to his neighbors, pouring it from the wineskin till they are drunk, so that he can gaze on their naked bodies. You will be filled with shame instead of glory. Now it is your turn! Drink and be exposed! The cup from the Lord's right hand is coming around to you, and disgrace will cover your glory. Habakkuk 2: 15, 16

Therefore do not be foolish, but understand what the Lord's will is. Do not get drunk on wine, which leads to debauchery. Instead, be filled with the Spirit. Ephesians 5:17, 18

They reeled and staggered like drunken men; they were at their wits' end. Psalm 107:27

Be careful, or your hearts will be weighed down with dissipation, drunkenness and the anxieties of life, and that day will close on you unexpectedly like a trap. Luke 21:34

The night is nearly over; the day is almost here. So let us put aside the deeds of darkness and put on the armor of light. Let us behave decently, as in the daytime, not in orgies and drunkenness, not in sexual immorality and debauchery, not in dissension and jealousy. Rather, clothe yourselves with the Lord Jesus Christ, and do not think about how to gratify the desires of the sinful nature. Romans 13:12-14

The acts of the sinful nature are obvious: sexual immorality, impurity and debauchery; idolatry and witchcraft; hatred, discord, jealousy, fits of rage, selfish ambition, dissensions, factions and envy; drunkenness, orgies, and the like. I warn you, as I did before, that those who live like this will not inherit the kingdom of God. Galatians 5:19-21

So then, let us not be like others, who are asleep, but let us be alert and self-controlled. For those who sleep, sleep at night, and those who get drunk, gets drunk at night. But since we belong to the day, let us be self-controlled, putting on faith and love as a breastplate, and the hope of salvation as a helmet. 1 Thessalonians 5:6-8

Since an overseer is entrusted with God's work, he must be blameless—not overbearing, not quick-tempered, not given to drunkenness, not violent, not pursuing dishonest gain. Titus 1:7

Appendix A: Biblical Quotes

For you have spent enough time in the past doing what pagans choose to do—living in debauchery, lust, drunkenness, orgies, carousing and detestable idolatry. 1 Peter 4:3

APPENDIX B: HELPFUL WEBSITES

http://www.gettingthemsober.com — Toby Rice Drews is, in my opinion, one of the most insightful author/counselors on the subject of alcoholism there is. Her website include videos, articles and a forum concerning alcoholism and ways to cope.

https://groups.yahoo.com/neo/groups/HopeForTodayGroup/info — This is an e-mail forum type group where people write of their experiences in an alcoholic relationship to encourage each other.

http://stepchat.com — This is a website with live Al-Anon, AA, and NA meetings. This is a wonderful site to go to when you can't get out of the house to go to a face-to-face meeting. There is also a "Friends and Family" room where you can talk live with people living in similar circumstances.

https://www.facebook.com/groups/LivingwAlcoholicsnAddicts — This is a Facebook group that is closed. You will have to request to get into it. It is affiliated with Al-Anon. It is a great place to go when you are at a low and need some encouragement from friends in the same situation. Also, you won't have to worry about your alcoholic getting into it and seeing your comments. It is not open to the public.

Appendix B: Helpful Websites

APPENDIX C: PHONING FOR HELP

Al-Anon Family Groups	1-888-425-2666
Alcohol Abuse and Crisis Intervention	1-800-234-0246
Alcohol and Drug Abuse Helpline and Treatment	1-800-234-0420
Alcohol and Drug Addiction Resource Center	1-800-390-4056
Alcoholic's Anonymous World Services, Inc.	1-212-870-3400
National Drug Information Treatment and Referral	1-800-662-4357
Cocaine National Hotline	1-800-262-2463
National Domestic Violence Hotline	1-800-799-7233
Domestic Violence Hotline	1-800-829-1122
STAND Against Domestic Violence	1-888-215-5555
Rape and Incest Hotline	1-800-656-4673
Suicide Hotline	1-800-273-8255
National Suicide Hotline	1-800-784-2433

Appendix C: Phoning for Help

APPENDIX D: DREAMS

Take my yoke upon you and learn from me, for I am gentle and humble in heart, and you will find rest for your souls. For my yoke is easy and my burden is light. Matthew 11: 29-30

I am no one special, but I have had three dreams that have profoundly affected my journey with an alcoholic. They have some pretty good messages, but whether you believe they were sent from God or not is totally up to you. I am certain He sent them to me when I needed them most – during very low times in my experience. I have debated whether to share them with anyone or not, but I think the messages are worth hearing anyway.

Dream #1

I am standing next to some random guy, and my husband is standing about 10 feet in front of us with his back to us.

I grabbed the man's arm next to me and yelled, "Quick! Stab him in the back while he's not looking! Kill him! He's spreading poison everywhere to everyone!" I was frantic.

Then the man turned to me, and I looked at him. That is when I realized the man was Jesus. He said to me, "No, _____ (my name), it's not _____ (my husband's name) that is spreading poison. Look down in front of him."

I looked. I saw something I hadn't seen before. In front of him on the ground was a huge snake lying on the ground.

"It's Satan in him that is spreading all the poison. Not, _____."

I woke up shaking, but with a new understanding. It wasn't my real husband that was acting this way. It was the result of Satan and his power over my husband, due to choices he had made, which led him into alcoholism and drug addiction. I looked at my husband in a different way after that. It was a relief to know that the old husband that I had fallen in

Appendix D: Dreams

love with and married was still in there somewhere. It gave me hope and a different perspective.

Dream #2

Fast-forward 4 years. My daughters and I had moved into my parents' home a week earlier. I was on an out of state business trip, and it was my last night in the hotel.

In my dream my family was living by the sea. My oldest daughter, now in college, was about age four again.

Apparently, a huge storm had hit our house. There were downed trees, broken limbs, pieces of wood from the torn up house and miscellaneous household debris all over the ground. My daughter and I began picking up pieces of wood and putting them into a pile to burn. Family was coming to visit, and we were trying to make the place look half-way presentable before they arrived.

Just then, my husband arrived. He began yelling at us. "Quit trying to run things. You're not doing what I tell you to do. You're always doing things your own way. Just do what I say!" He bent down and was screaming right into my daughter's scared face. Her little body was trembling.

I stood there looking on in disbelief. Not believing what I was seeing.

Suddenly, there was a huge shooting star shooting across the sky over the ocean, falling down toward the horizon. It hit the ground and there was a huge explosion.

I said, "Watch this, _____ (daughter's name)!" I knew in my heart it was our salvation — our help in a time of trouble. We looked on very excited and happy. My husband stopped yelling and looked toward the horizon.

Then, out of the explosion, Jesus came running toward us over the water — except it was more like he was floating straight toward us — moving very fast. His arms were open wide. He was smiling. Ready to engulf us with his care.

In the background a song was playing like in a movie, "It's time to runaway, runaway, runaway..."

Appendix D: Dreams

My husband shrank back into the shadows. My daughter and I looked on joyously for our salvation drew nigh.

I woke up crying with relief. God was with me. I immediately understood the meaning.

The storm that had torn up our home and our family was really the result my husband's alcoholism and drug addiction had had on our family. The emotional abuse my children and I endured was not excusable and didn't make sense, but God was sending help. Jesus would be with us. He loved us and wouldn't leave us alone in our flight to get away. I knew now that I had God's blessing and care in separating my children and myself from this situation.

I got up and went to I-tunes trying to find the song that I heard playing in the background. I couldn't find the exact song, but found the song with the closest words, vocal sounds and instrumental sounds I could. When I downloaded it. I couldn't believe the words I was hearing. Panima is the name of the group that sang the song called "Runaway." It was as if God was speaking directly to me. I broke down and sobbed at the awesomeness of God's unfathomable love for me.

I don't know anything about the young people that sing this song, but I do know that God can use anyone to help someone else. God bless them. You can find the words online. They're amazing.

Dream #3

My dream started by my trying to get some guy to like me by solving all his problems (he had a broken ankle). I told him I knew where he could go to get it fixed, what doctor to go to, how he could pay for it, how he should get it fixed, and that I could drive him there.

Apparently, I was living in a multi-story building like a hotel. I began looking through all the rooms for my room; so, I could get my car key to drive this person to a doctor. I began looking through all the rooms, but couldn't find mine. As I looked I became more and more agitated. Finally, when I had searched through all of the rooms in the whole building, I came to the last one. By that time, I was very stressed and ready to give up.

I looked into the last room. It was dark, but I could make out the outline of a man dressed in a white shirt, pants and shoes. I told him my

Appendix D: Dreams

problem. I needed to find my room; so, I could get my key to drive this man to the doctor's office.

All of the sudden, I realized it was Jesus. He looked at me all patient and sad. He said, "Why do you try to take care of everything on your own and go through all of this pain, when you could have come to me in the beginning? I can show you the way and save you from all of this misery."

Then, I awoke to a new life. The burden of my taking care of all my husband's problems in order for him to like me, and for me to feel accepted, was gone. I suddenly realized, that it wasn't my place to try to get someone to like me by solving his or her problems. That was God's job, not mine. Suddenly, I knew I was to give the load I had been carrying totally to Jesus. This I do daily and on some days many times a day. Praise the Lord.

Dream #4

I dreamed that I was driving down a straight road with my two daughters. It was a long drive. I was in that zone you get into when you aren't really paying attention to the road or your surroundings. You are just moving forward.

Along the road there were monsters jumping up and down doing tricks, trying to get my attention. There were also road signs that I paid no attention to as well. I just kept moving forward in kind of a daze. I was confident the road would take me to where I wanted to be.

Then, the road moved upward over a large body of water, as if it were turning into a bridge. Suddenly, the road ended. Just like that, our car was flying into thin air. Down it came with a splash into the water. Quickly I got my daughters unbuckled. I rolled down a window and pushed them out into the chilly water. They new how to swim, but I saw it was a long way to the shore. The water was choppy. I didn't know if we could make it so far. I was so scared.

Fortunately, I noticed three strong men swimming in the water nearby. They seemed to know how to swim so easily — a different way than we were swimming. I asked them to show us how to swim that way; so we could get to the shore safely.

Appendix D: Dreams

The man by me said he would show us how to swim like them, but he said, "You know you wouldn't have had to go through this, if you had paid attention to the signs."

"What signs?" I asked.

"The ones all along the road. They were everywhere trying to get your attention, but you ignored them."

Then, I began to understand. I had caused my children and myself to suffer, because I had ignored the signs all along the road of life. There were so many times when God had tried to get may attention to change my course of action, but I always thought I had it all figured out, but I didn't. Lord, have mercy.

Once again, I had messed up by thinking I knew best. How many ways did God need to tell me that I needed to quit trying to fix things on my own? That I needed to look to him for the answers?

Watch for the signs. Got it.

And so, those were my dreams. Maybe, they were from God, maybe from eating pizza too late at night. I'm not sure, but I do know I learned some valuable lessons from them. I hope they benefited you, too.

God be with us all…

CPSIA information can be obtained at www.ICGtesting.com
Printed in the USA
LVOW10s1336290816

502319LV00035B/760/P